Creative Writing in Prose

Creative Writing in Prose

Marjorie Oludhe Macgoye

University of Nairobi Press

First published 2009 by
University of Nairobi Press
Jomo Kenyatta Memorial Library, University of Nairobi
P.O. Box 30197 – 00100 Nairobi
E-mail:nup@uonbi.ac.ke
Website:http://www.uonbi.ac.ke/press/

The University of Nairobi Press supports and promotes University of Nairobi's objectives of discovery, dissemination and preservation of knowledge, and stimulation of intellectual and cultural life by publishing works of highest quality in association with partners in different parts of the world. In doing so, it adheres to the University's tradition of excellence, innovation and scholarship.

The moral rights of the author have been asserted.

University of Nairobi Library CIP Data

PE 1425 .M3 808.81 dc 20	Macgoye, Marjorie Oludhe Creative Writing in Prose/Marjorie M. Oludhe – Nairobi: University of Nairobi Press, 2009. 135p. 1. Creative writing–Tradition 2. Creative writing–Narrative I. Title

ISBN 9966 846 83 2

Printed by
Starbright Services Ltd
P.O. Box 66949 – 00200
Nairobi

Contents

Preface

I am grateful to the Administration, Literature Department and students of Egerton University for inviting me to take part in the lectures and discussions on which these pages are based. In particular, I want to thank Professor Emilia, Ilieva for over-ruling my doubts and bringing her fine, polyglot scholarship to bear on issues which have crept up out of the shadows to discomfit us older writers who used to be sure we knew where we were going. That does not mean that the way to that destination was ever easy or direct as John Donne wrote in his third Satire, more than 400 years ago:

> On a huge hill,
> Cragged and steep, Truth stands and he that will
> Reach her, about must, and about must go,
> And what the hill's suddenness resists, win so; (Donne,
> 116)

I hope that these pages may help us to see how, over the years, storytellers have found means to "by indirections, find directions out", and what safeguards are available to keep the reader with them.

There are no "set books" here. I believe all the personal favourites I have quoted are found in Kenyan libraries or bookshops. The fellowship of book-lovers is such that I am sure readers will be assisted to find other books by the same authors or from the same generation if these have dropped from the shelves. Wide reading is essential for creative writers, but wide observation and conversation even more so.

Many promising writers drop from view because they buy a car and whiz past the street-corner where a story is taking shape and waiting to be noticed. A story is not stereotyped into an "issue" or a "problem." The "exile story", the "growing up story", the "generation conflict story" are not genres, only stereotypes: a valid story is in some particular way, one of its kind. Try it and see.

Under *References* on page 121, there is a list of works referred to in the text. Some of the novels listed have gone through many editions. The edition quoted is the one referred to. Therefore, I have avoided giving page numbers unless the edition is also named. This is not a list of prescribed reading, though I hope the book will attract your interest to some of the stories frequently quoted. The practising writer has to read just as the practising footballer has to watch other people's games and study the technique. One novel a week for life would be the barest minimum. As a rough guide, I should say that the Kenyan writer or student should be familiar with at least 50 Kenyan novels, at least one (original or translated) from each other African country (though just a few do not appear on the standard lists), at least one English novel from the 18th century and one from each decade from 1820 to the present, at least ten American novels, six Indian novels in English and three each from Australia, France, Germany and South America.

However, since we cannot know whether the great novel of the century will be published in *Fiji* or *Uzbekistan* next week, perhaps the best policy is just to keep looking for this great novel.

Marjorie Oludhe Macgoye,
Nairobi, Kenya

Acknowledgements

I am grateful to Philip Ochieng' for permission to reprint the passage from his column in *The Sunday Nation* of 10th August, 2003.

After many attempts, we have not been able to trace the copyright holder of Daniachew Worku's *The Thirteenth Sun* in the African Writers Series.

Chapter *1*

Writing in Prose

Our subject is *creative writing in prose*. I hope you know the story of *Le Bourgeois Gentilhomme*. This comedy by the seventeenth century French dramatist, Moliere, has been translated into Swahili under the title *Mchuuzi Mungwana*. Monsieur Jourdain, having made a lot of money through trade, desires to become a gentleman according to the elaborate manners of Moliere's time. He therefore engages a language master who teaches him that speech and writing can be divided into prose and poetry. "Poetry is a special form of language, but prose is ordinary speech, what you are saying every day". M. Jourdain is delighted. "How clever I am!" he cries. "All my life I have been speaking prose and never knew it."

Well, you, the reader, are equally clever because you have been speaking prose from your earliest years. One of the most striking and mystifying experiences of family life is to watch a young child learning the codes of speech in one language or more than one within about three years. It is a very complex operation.

I remember one of my grandsons, just over three, remarking *"Mtoto ametapika"* (The baby has vomited) and then *"Mama ametapikiwa na mtoto."* (Mother has been vomited on by the baby). This would have taken me a long time to work out when I was learning the Swahili language as an adult.

My own children were used to our telling them everything twice, once in Luo and once in English. They seldom got mixed up. But I remember one day when there was a storm brewing, George, at two, calling out, "Look, mama, it is going to *koth*." Untypically, he had translated the English verb *rain* into the Luo noun *koth*. Children frequently learn correct forms by imitation – *buy, bought, go, went*. A few years later, as their vocabulary grows, they try to rationalise by applying an inappropriate model – *buy, buyed, go, goed*.

Adults also sometimes lose ground to an inappropriate model – *she/he* instead of *he* or *they, demise* instead of *death, resource person* instead of *assistant, inappropriate* instead of *sinful*.

What has this to do with learning to write creatively in English? A great deal. First, it tells us that it is not only possible, but an everyday experience to acquire perfect idiomatic command of a language. We have all done it at least once. We can do it again, though the first experience is so overwhelming that it may for a time interfere with the learning of a second language, especially if we do not have perfect models. When I say "perfect", I am not referring to the grammar-book standard of correctness which will reply "it is *I*, Mary" when asked who is speaking or introduce "This is the sister *whom* I told you about". These forms are no longer required in everyday speech. I am talking about complete fluency in conveying your meaning to a wide variety of English speakers. I am told that the late Bishop Alf Stanway, when he had just arrived in East Africa, stood up to deliver his first sermon in the old St. Stephen's Church, Nairobi, on Boxing Day, which in the church calendar, is St. Stephen's Day. So, like any other good Australian, he announced, "Todye is St Stephen's Dye" and the interpreter immediately translated, *"Kufa ni kufa kwake Stefano Mtakatifu."* This translates the Australian pronunciation of *day* as meaning *die*. In a few years, however, the preacher became a completely fluent speaker of Swahili, and away from Australia, his English became a little moderated too. We shall discuss later some of the ways in which this moderation occurs.

When I left Dar es Salaam, I handed over management of the University Bookshop to a young woman who was the first ever Barabaig to get a degree. The first male student from the area was coming along a couple of years later. Clara's father was a Barabaig but her mother spoke Iraqw, a click language. Both of these were languages which at the time had very few English speakers who could act as interpreters or informants. So, she was a treasure to the linguistics department, where she studied French. And yet she had mastered the two parental languages before ever going to school.

Second, the observation of first language learning tells us that thorough acquaintance with the structures (which is not the same thing as being able to name them) helps us to meet various situations. It is not very often that we need to use an expression like *kutapika* in the passive voice, *kutapikiwa*, but once we understand the formation and use of the passive, it becomes possible. At university level, we need to verbalise in all subjects, and whether or not budding authors have studied linguistics as a subject, they need to be able to analyse the kinds of clauses, phrases, participles and parts of speech which are the raw material of writing.

I remember Professor Okoth Okombo, the linguist, telling me that when he went to college, he was amazed to find that there were names for all the different strokes in swimming which every child from Rusinga Island performed without giving them a thought. An urban child learns them one after the other by name. Perhaps the same is true of parts of speech in the mother tongue. Nonetheless, the teacher of a language, like the teacher of swimming, needs to be able to break down the subject into components.

The teaching of basic writing skills, which every educated person needs, is not the same as the teaching of creative writing. It is possible to teach how a novel is written or how a dull report or a passage of history can be made memorable. To teach someone to *do* it is another matter, and *doing it* is not compulsory in real life.

I can watch hour after hour, a cookery demonstrator making beef strogonov and explaining her methods. Without doubt, I shall learn how she makes beef strogonov. But experience in the kitchen tells me that I probably, shall never be able to do it right. My family needs not go hungry because I wont do it right. There are other dishes. In all areas of life, enough is enough. So, let us look at some of the elements of writing good, flexible prose and how they relate to the making of literature.

Notionally, we all have a choice of language, that is, everybody has a choice, both of register within the mother tongue or language of instruction, and of other learned languages. For practical purposes, the Kenyan system, for instance, requires students to write in English. Learning to do so well will inform the student's creative writing in any other language he may adopt. I speak and write in English, not gender-speak. For me, *he* in English is the nominative pronoun for an unspecified person, just as *a-* is in Swahili or *o-* in Dholuo. If you need to specify a female person, there are means of doing so, and, if you do not, it is easy to turn the statement into the plural, which in English is gender-specific, even in appearance. Further, because English does not have cases, as in German, or construct possessives as in Dholuo, prepositions or other joining words are often needed to show how words are related to one another. In English, *Mother Mary* does not mean "Mary's mother," but a mother whose name is Mary. Something strange has happened recently to the Kenyan usage of possessives in English. An organization can write to members, *Please find enclosed seminars' invitations*. Well, the seminars are not the issuers of invitations but the subject of them. One would expect *Please find our invitations to the seminars.* The apostrophe is usually reserved for animate beings or collectives.

Here is an example of seminar-speak taken from a local newspaper. There is no punctuation mark other than the full stop:

> Analysts expect the failure to register progress on a
> drastic reduction of trade distorting domestic support and
> a phase out of export subsidies to dominate negotiations
> on agricultural reform.

The meaning appears to be, "Analysts expect failure in certain areas to dominate negotiations." This makes sense, but one does not ordinarily negotiate from failure to failure. Let us analyse the sentence further:

What is "progress on a drastic reduction of trade"? It seems to imply that it is a good thing to reduce trade. And it is *trade* that distorts domestic support? If I were editing the passage, I should ask if I might insert a hyphen between *trade* and *distorting* thus changing the whole sense. Now, the *failure* could be failure to reduce subsidies on First World commodities, that is, *trade-distorting domestic support*. If this is correct, in line with the author's intention, then *phase-out* would also logically become a hyphenated word. But it is still not clear whether *phase-out of export subsidies* is one of the things somebody has failed to register progress in or whether it is something that has already happened and will dominate negotiations. We have no sign other than the absence of a comma to tell us whether *and* joins *failure* and *a phase-out* or *reduction* and *a phase-out*. Thus, this kind of careless writing leaves the reader uncertain about what is happening on one or other side of the negotiations. No professional writer can afford to be that careless.

It is a simple rule that a conjunction joins two items of similar kind and weight – two nouns, two phrases, two clauses and so on. In the example "I ordered fish and chips and then asked for a cup of tea" the first *"and"* joins two nouns and the second joins two clauses. Neither may be omitted.

In every language, there are permitted variants of style, register and sentence structure, but there are certain parts of speech that need to be defined, and punctuation marks that are road signs as to how the passage is to be read. There are different conventions about punctuation, historically and between England and America. However, the distinctions between words and idioms are more than a convention, and it is necessary to recognise the standard forms even if you are using a dialect. This is as true of a Kenyan writing in English as it is of the Irish Samuel Beckett, who chooses to write in French, or the Pole, Joseph Conrad, who adopted English as the language of his books after considering the alternative of French. Isaac Bashevis Singer, a Nobel Prize winner, chose to go on writing in Yiddish even when Yiddish-speaking communities were dispersed after the chaos of the Second World War. A group of Jewish writers had already decided to write creative works in Hebrew before anyone spoke it as a domestic language. Before the twentieth century, it was mostly a language of prayer and scripture reading.

In all these cases, there had to be a norm for the language against which any intentional deviation could be explained. When Chinua Achebe visited Kenya and was asked about his opinions on mother-tongue writing, he replied that everyone had a choice, but it would not be useful for him to speak in Kenya if there were no a common tongue – namely English – in which he could be understood

Many of us have difficulty in making certain sounds or tones. I find it very difficult to control tones, but even if our pronunciation is imperfect, it should still differentiate sounds, and this is particularly important for English teachers. How we speak affects how we write, and it is distressing to find in newspapers confusing *cause* and *course*, *lose* and *loose*, *differ* and *defer*. If you make a mistake in spelling *accommodation*, it is shameful but it does not prevent the reader knowing what you mean. But if you confuse *sell* with *sale, defect* with *deflect; lead* with *lid,* your meaning is lost.

Bad is not the same as *bird*. *Anger* is not the same as *hunger*. *Cat* is not the same as *cut*. *Another man* (that is, the second) is not the same as *a man*. *Relevant* has no meaning unless we are told what is relevant to what. *I did my hair* is not the same as *I had my hair done*. A *matchbox* is not the same as a *box (full) of matches*. *Some time* is very different indeed from *sometimes*. *I don't care* is (for English but not American speakers) very different from *I don't mind*. *Sweet* is not the same as *nice* or *tasty*, when referring to food. On the other hand, English does not distinguish between a maternal and paternal aunt or between an older or younger brother. Extra words are needed to express these distinctions. The more ways we can find to make a correct and unambiguous statement the more eloquent we are likely to be.

Ugandan students once asked me whether I produced creative writing in Dholuo or Swahili. This made me pause for thought, since they said that fifty years should be enough for one to master a language. I do not write professionally in either language, though I write personal letters in both and give addresses in both at weddings and funerals. The plain fact is that we all do some things and not others. I know how to book theatre tickets but not how to order a round of drinks. A person may watch football but play only tennis. I can go through the Athanasian creed in Swahili but can describe the symptoms of measles more accurately in Dholuo. I cannot give the rules for the game of *bao* which has no English name, as far as I know, in any language. We can be more or less eloquent according to the effort we put into a particular area, but none of us is omniscient. There is nothing to be ashamed of in specialising in a particular form or subject matter.

Now, let us be very careful here. Creative writing in Kenya is ordinarily taught in English, occasionally in the Swahili language, as a matter of convenience. Imaginative work can be done in any language, using its resources of cadence and idiom. In my view, students should be able to offer assignments in any language, but an assessor must be found competent to mark them. But the plea for accuracy and logical development is not language-dependent. It can be taught in the language of instruction, along with story construction, the planned release of information to the reader and devices for beginning and ending a story.

One symptom of failing to distinguish the functions and relationship of parts of speech is the use of headlines that fail to connect words together, and which would not have been allowed a generation ago. Once a column head in the Nation read *Food Poison Students Now Leave Hospital.* What does this mean?

There are two ways of testing the linguistic validity of a statement, that is, whether it makes unambiguous sense (which is not to say whether it is fair or truthful). You can translate it into another language or test it by substituting other words in the same categories of grammar. So you could try, "Mathematics students now leave hospital" or "history students" do the same, assuming that the column below will explain the circumstances. In this analogy "food poison students" means students of food poisoning. But who studies food poisoning? This is just a tiny bit of the medical syllabus. You do not refer to literature students as *Concubine* students or *Aminata* students. You could also try to alter the punctuation: *Food Poison(ing):* (colon) *Students now leave hospital.* However, it would be in every way simpler to rearrange the statement: *students suspected of suffering from food poisoning now leave hospital;* or; *victims of food poisoning discharged.* Another example is "Somali herdsmen Order". Is *order* a noun or a verb? Is order given to the herdsmen or by them? The passage indicates that Somali herdsmen, only of a certain area were ordered to move to another named area while a fixed location was being negotiated. A better headline would be *Somali Herders Moved.*

Short sentences introduce a topic. Longer ones are needed to develop it. In practice, we often break-up our sentences into phrases or explanations (a phrase is a meaningful group of words without a finite verb) but in such cases, it should always be possible to reconstruct the grammatical statement by inserting the missing items. Writers should always have a reference book on grammar at hand and test their sentences by substitution. We may hear, "What a lot of fuss (she is making) over nothing (of any importance)". An exclamation like "never no more" may express *"(I) (intend) never (to do it any) more."*

Controlling the structure of our sentences can help us make fine distinctions. Listen to the following:

> When he finished the work, he went home.
> On account of finishing work early, he found the buses were not crowded.
> Having finished work, he was given leave to go.
> Finishing his work early, he was able to read the newspaper.
> Although he finished work early, he was not allowed to leave.
> Finishing his work early was a matter of pride to him
> His finishing work early was seen by his boss as a reason to give him more to do.

These are just a few of the *constructions* using *finish* as a verb or a noun. We can also speak of the *finish* of a fine work of craftsmanship. Many people will tell you that there is a virtue in writing short sentences. This is not true, though we have to avoid adding extra words that do not contribute to the meaning. If you reduced any of the expressions quoted above to two simple sentences, *He finished his work. He went home,* you would leave out an important part of the meaning. How, *why* and *when*, actions relate to each other is an essential part of statement. To read works of earlier centuries, you need to know forms like "lest we forget" and "had he remembered" (just as I was expected to learn *"naisipokuwa, usipokuwa, tusipokuwa"*). But nowadays, these forms are hardly used outside examination papers. In real life, we say "in case we forget" or "if he had remembered". Generally, we write down what we can get our tongue round in speaking. We do not talk like our grandfathers any more than we dress like them, but we can quote what they used to say as we recognise in a photograph what they used to look like when they were younger.

Anyone, in any language, may pause to search for the best word. This is a requirement Kenyans share with mother-tongue speakers of English. The old adage is true in any language – easy writing is damned hard reading. To make a good impression with the written word demands an effort. This is equally true when we are writing in dialect or, where necessary, in jargon. This is not just a lazy option. It is a way of giving characters their distinct voices and this sometimes amounts to putting over a point of view. Dialect is a way of talking that relates to community of location or social class. It often exists along with perfect fluency in the standard language. But there are local usages. For example, I suspect it is only in Kenya that the single English word "Imagine..." can constitute a complete evocative sentence.

Jargon is a way of talking that refers to an occupation or a hobby. *Over, Roger, Wilco,* are terms that belong to radio-communication. *In, out, bowled, fielded, eleven, pitch* is jargon that belongs to the game of cricket. They may be used as images of other activities, but in ordinary conversation, the speaker is expected to use standard forms.

Occasionally, a writer may wish to limit the point of view to the extent of putting the narrative in dialect even if some of the characters speak in a different register. Arthur Flowers and Cormac McCarthy are among the American writers who do this extremely well. In doing it, they presuppose that there is an audience either sensitive to that particular speech pattern or sufficiently familiar with the rules of deviation to get the sense.

People create for themselves the words they need. In my childhood, there were no words for *computer, cellotape, nylon, cassette, photocopy, supersonic, genome.* There was nothing for such words to refer to. Sometimes, people distort existing words in preference to thinking of new ones that mean what they want to say. *Gender*, for instance, is defined in the 1975 revised edition of the *Shorter Oxford English Dictionary* as "each of the three (or two) grammatical 'kinds' corresponding more or less to difference of sex (or absence of sex) into which substantives are discriminated." Substantive is the technical term for certain kinds of noun. So up to thirty years ago, *gender* was remotely connected to the idea of sex but even today, it cannot by any stretch of imagination be made to mean *woman*.

Like M. Jourdain, we have been speaking prose all our lives. What does that leave us to learn about it? Well, plenty. First, we already have several styles of speaking. We all know that we do not talk to little children in the same words we use for our age-mates, parents or teachers. This is called distinguishing the *register* of speech.

In writing, we vary the register according to whether we are writing a popular magazine story, a letter to an MP, a school essay or a personal letter. To adopt an appropriate register for literary writing needs thought, it needs knowledge and it needs time.

Generally, the work of writing is hard and time-consuming because every item is a fresh start. There are a few exceptions. Popeye cartoons, for example, have been going on for about 65 years now, talking about food and family relationships, so the dialogue writer has very little freedom of choice.

I don't find it easy to write children's stories, like *The Black Hand Gang*, but once the first set of characters are established, with their social conditions, there is a starting point from which new situations can be developed. This puts a limitation on the way the story can grow, but it offers a framework within which the memory of both reader and writer can operate.

You are probably studying *creative writing* because you are good at English, and you wonder why I am making such a fuss about it. Isn't instinct and the feel for a rhetorical sentence enough to get on by? I sometimes ask myself this same question. I used to get good marks and scholarships. I write in my mother tongue. Though my forebears did not have advanced formal education, they included good talkers and singers. I have eleven books in print. Yet, I still have manuscripts rejected up to this day and letters to the press ignored.

We must not take literature as an easy option. It requires as much rigorous attention as any other subject of study, though the reading may give more pleasure. We may do quite well by instinct in the first draft of a piece of writing, just as we may make a rough cast of a calculation before resorting to pencil and paper. The square of 5.5, for instance, must lie somewhere between 25, which is the square of 5 and 36, which is the square of 6. Any numerate person knows that. But the answer to a sum requires more precision than that, and one must be able to show the working. So it is with the analysis of a sentence. There is no calculator to pass or fail your writing. You are out there alone to convince your audience like the stand-up comedian on the stage.

Technology changes all the time. Any printer of my age must have been astonished when he first found out that words could be printed from typing done on a keyboard instead of being inserted letter by letter into a container called a "form". Any change done in the process required the typesetter to alter all the subsequent lines up to the end of a paragraph or beyond. Therefore, a book would be "out of print" when those racks of words, lines and pages were dispersed. The older printers in Nairobi can still show visitors the hardware that was used in setting up letterpress. Not so many authors are willing to reveal the stages of revision and paste-up their works have undergone. Yet, the principles of composition remain the same whether you trace the letters with a stick on wet clay or dictate them over a telephone in the middle of a battle. That is why I tend to be sceptical of excessive reliance on machines.

A word processor is a valuable tool for the final stages of typesetting. The danger involved is that the proofreader may jump from one mistake needing correction to the next marked on the draft without checking all the consequent changes of pronouns, tenses and punctuation. If you copy your pages manually, as I have always done, you will find that in every case – including the lecture on which this chapter is based – there are slips to be corrected and improvements to be made whether it is the third transcription or the seventh. So if you are using a computer, *please* do not make alterations of style (as distinct from just correcting spelling) on the screen but save a printout of the original, because there was always a reason, even if you have now forgotten it, for choosing the original word and order of points. Any change must be made consistently.

Even after you have mastered your vocabulary, grammar, and register, you still have to consider balance and euphony – pleasant sound – in prose, and how it affects the reader. Sentences should be rounded and rhythmic unless a shock effect is intended. Yet in prose, even a strong rhythm does not have the framing effect that helps us to memorise lines of verse, so we cannot lay down exact rules borne out by classical examples. Only the co-ordination of parts should be logical and repetition of words and structures can be used for rhetorical effect.

In prose as in poetry, there are styles appropriate to different periods and approaches. Some are narrative, some argumentative, some persuasive, and they may be addressed to a popular audience, an academic or an artistic group. Each item has its tactics for seizing the reader's attention. You are probably familiar with the "I have a dream" speech of Martin Luther King Jr. .This is a great example of rhetoric. Camara Laye's *The African Child*, originally written in French, is an autobiography with a magical narrative quality, and something entirely new in African literature of the 1950s. Questions since raised about Laye's methods in no way diminish the beauty of his prose.

David Shenk's book *Justice, Reconciliation and Peace in Africa* is a great and entirely readable expository book. You would hardly recognise it as the work of an American professor unless you knew that the writer's parents were missionaries in a Tanzanian village and he grew up strongly influenced by the vocabulary of the Revival Fellowship.

No book is easy to write. A textbook may be easier than others, if the writer has a laid down syllabus and is aware of what the students are supposed to know at the beginning. When it comes to expounding a subject, especially one involving new research, not for an agreed syllabus but for the world market, this is a much more delicate task. The same is true of learned journals where the readership is scholarly and in certain contexts even words we think we know like "material", "animal" or "classical" take on a new and specialised meaning. The only way to aspire to such heights is to read in depth, read, and read, noting every comma and looking up every word that does not seem to make sense, believing that there has to be a logical meaning which will one day dawn on us.

You do not go to study music without knowing tonic solfa and the pentatonic or other scales, which occur in your birthright culture. Yet, some Kenyan students say they find difficulty in following the richly textured classical sentences of a writer like Chinua Achebe. Here is such a sentence from *Anthills of the Savannah:* (p. 102 in the Heinemann Kenya edition):

> She came down in the resplendent Pillar of Water, remembered now in legend only, but stumbled upon, some say, by the most fortunate in rare conditions of sunlight, rarer even than the eighteen-year cycle of Odunke festivals and their richly arrayed celebrants leading garlanded cattle in procession through village pathways to sacrifice.

I do not think there are any English words here that college students do not know. The Odunke festival in Nigeria might need a note. The main clause is *She came down* (she being the goddess or spirit) and all the rest of the sentence describes the *Pillar of Water* in which she is manifested and a comparison between the rarity of the conditions of sunlight in which the *Pillar* is glimpsed and the eighteen-year cycle of sacrificial festivals. The second finite verb, *say*, is part of the complex of description relating to the *Pillar*.

A student of literature has to be able to trace the connections just as a student of dentistry will spot and accurately record the weak places in your teeth. Without this observation, correct treatment is impossible.

When you attend weddings or funerals or dowry meetings at your home places, I am sure you will hear, and on occasion, will pronounce, sentences quite as intricate as this one, with the same rhetorical force and the same communal involvement. In fact, you should be able to translate Achebe's sentence into whatever language you use on those occasions. You have to bring to the study of literature, and even more to the performance of literature, everything you have got, and go on looking for more experience to bring to it.

Journalism is not subordinate to creative writing. It is a highly skilled profession in which many Kenyans excel. Fast and fluent writing is just one aspect of it. The writer of a novel or short story usually has to search for a publisher over months and years, and then take advice from an editor. But a newspaper story will go stale if it is not accepted at once, and there is hardly ever a second chance, since competing papers are trying to hold the reader's interest in topical events.

The journalist must be able to gather facts with speed and accuracy, mindful of the legal hazards. He must be conscious of the limited space available and tolerant with editors who insist on changing titles (but not too tolerant, we hope, of careless typesetting). Much of the work is quickly forgotten, but a few pieces may be collected and help to form public opinion or be quoted as an emblem of the time. Good journalists read widely and this can help them practice brevity of expression and find memorable catch phrases. More leisured writers, in their turn, can profitably study journalists' techniques in evoking public emotion and putting side-by-side pieces of information that illuminate one another even without a cause and effect link.

Often, the most memorable and innovative item in the newspaper is the political cartoon. It has a very short shelf life, but it conveys the essence of pages in print. Only rarely does a historian immortalise such a piece as typical or quote an advertisement. But its influence is incalculable. The man who modelled the Sloan's Liniment advertisement would not have believed that a century later he would be admired by old ladies all over Africa as *Masherubu*. You never know your luck.

I can only give some hints as you forge your own style by trial and error. Go straight into the statement, avoiding vague introductions like "It is commonly thought that" or "as we explained previously". Make sure your sentence is complete with a finite verb (one defined by person and number). Casual phrases like "green leaves and red flowers" can be permitted only in the most conversational styles, but there are always exceptions. The statement must always be complete – a sentence like "give the medicine" or "tilapia live in water", is grammatically correct but does not mean much unless it is filled out: "Give the medicine three times a day after meals," "Tilapia live in fresh water, typically in the Rift Valley lakes."

The argument or narrative should progress logically or emotionally, preferably both. The relationship between statements is shown either by conjunctions – "New blue Omo washes whiter and it shows," or by punctuation – "Go to the reception desk: you will be shown where to report." Come to the end and then stop. Make sure descriptive material is firmly attached where it belongs – "Being hungry, he finished the chicken," not "Being hungry, the chicken got finished." Watch out for tense sequence but trust your ear: there is a subtle difference between "Since I was a keen student, I was surprised" and "Since I am a keen student, I was surprised."

Always read aloud any passage of your writing that bothers you, to see if it sounds clumsy or ambiguous. Do not be afraid to repeat a word that is essential to your meaning. This is better style than introducing periphrasis, roundabout ways of avoiding repetition like "the former," the newcomer." Your final resource is to read and read, analyse, criticise and read some more of the excellent examples available in all places and times. Thomas Traherne, a 17th century clergyman, wrote some of the loveliest sentences in English prose. They were not published until 1908, when the manuscript was found mixed with some old volumes in a bookshop in Charing Cross Road, London. You never know what treasures you may come across, or when your own treasured compositions will be discovered in their turn. Just keep writing.

Chapter 2

Creative Writing in the Literary Tradition

Our subject is *creative writing in prose*, so we must give a working definition of literature and the place of new writing within it. Literature is an area of practice and experience which can be studied like any other subject. Shall we take medicine as an example of the way all subjects change in detail? The doctors who treated me as a child had never heard of antibiotics. They did not yet exist. The dentist would put a gas mask over the patient's face to take away the pain of having a tooth out. There were no injections to freeze the gum. In spite of this, our grannies knew that the mould from a rotten potato could heal a cut, though they did not know the name penicillin. People in Zanzibar knew the anaesthetics properties of clove oil. Yet, the doctors and dentists covered the same ground – anatomy, physiology, therapeutics, surgery – as they do today. So with literature, there are new terms, techniques and tastes, but the art of *making* something out of words has been known for millennia. Ancient clay tablets from what is now Iraq show that at one period, a completely different language was used for literary and historical texts from that used in making public administrative announcements.

We need to learn about what already exists in literature and about the techniques, which can prepare us both for our own writing and for evaluating new works as they come to be written by others.

There are different definitions of what literature is. Obviously, not all the written words that come out in newspapers, magazines, instruction manuals for cars, textbooks, stories and verses can be regarded as literature in the sense of the subject. Nevertheless we may talk of "the literature of accountancy" in the same way as we talk about "the tools of the stone-mason," as being something subservient to another art or trade. As a working definition, we can say that literature in prose is a statement, whether literal or fictional, that is memorable and shapely enough to remain significant beyond the context of its original time and place.

For historical or biographical research non-literary pieces of writing, advertisements and price-lists, newspaper articles, jokes and recipes may be extremely useful. They indicate the background of experience and the origins of words. *Muoroto, piny owacho, manowari, pesa nane, koscreenwo, komerera*, relate to times which already may need a historical explanation. Looking into these matters gives greater depth to reading and analysis. But when we are reading stories as literary artefacts, in which the balance and weight of the parts is a major factor, we must, to a great extent, assume that the author has done his own spadework and indicated what the reader needs to know. We do not need to annotate every breed of horse or dog or every make of vehicle. Kenyans empathise with the British cartoon character Flo Capp without, perhaps, ever having been in a bingo hall or placed a bet on a racetrack.

Some critics say that a classic is what is still being read twenty years after it first came out. They may be right, though certain non-literary works like *Napoleon's Book of Fate* or *How to Make*

Friends and Influence People by Dale Carnegie go on much longer than that.

Any literary work Kenyans produced in the year 2003 is going to be coloured by our feelings about the National Alliance Rainbow Coalition (NARC) government, the deaths of the Vice-President and of Whispers, and the war in Iraq looming in the distance. This makes it different from a textbook of accountancy or a manual of car repair, which only occasionally need to refer to a technical change. The novel will not be read in twenty years time unless the author has been able either to tone down these references into a longer perspective or to make them so vivid and detailed that they recreate the feeling of the day. By doing this in a novel or a play, the writer brings to the reader's mind similar feelings and decisions experienced in his own time, and shows how they have been absorbed into history.

One novelist who is particularly good at this is the American E.L. Doctorow, from whom I personally have learned a lot. I am sure his novels are going to continue being read when many chronicles of the immediate scene have been forgotten. I am not saying there is anything wrong with reading topical novels like Wahome Mutahi's *Doomsday* or *Black Gold of Chepkube* by Wamugunda Geteria. Telling a good story is half the battle for a fiction writer. But remember that it often takes a bit of time to separate what you get from a book from what you know already, and what another reader may not know. So, if you take Francis Imbuga's novel *Shrine of Tears*, which I believe to be a very good one, as an example, it represents a situation which has already changed. I am well acquainted with the Kenya National Theatre of 1970s and 80s and its surroundings. I remember the shock of the death of the actress Stella Muka on University Way. I also remember her amazing stage performances. But the test of the novel is whether those who were not there can see and hear almost as vividly what the place was like, what controversies and motivations operated, the feeling of the time.

Non-fiction works also need additional explanation and documentation as time goes on. I have even heard a pause in a funeral eulogy when the young people present needed an explanation of the word *jukebox*. Try to recall the novels you have enjoyed that made you feel present in the time and place they depict. These will be models for your future writing.

Our aim in studying creative writing is not primarily to create great works. Even in bigger and more developed countries, people do not expect to come across a great novel or a great piece of music or a great scientific discovery every year. Groups may come together which nurture excellence in one form or another and then change or dissolve. The Zomba campus of the University of Malawi used to be called "a nest of singing birds," the same figure of speech used to describe the lyrical outpouring in England of the 1590s. But many of the Malawian poets have since dispersed. People work at shaping the themes that interest them. A few of the works get published, but in all countries, the majority do not, and the public gains extra insight by comparing the private writings of the people they know with what is in print.

Creative writing in prose is usually taken to mean novels and short stories. But there is not really a hard and fast line between fiction and other kinds of narrative that are meant to arouse feeling and reflection in the reader – autobiography, biography, travel writing, social history and the arts, essays, which can include serious pieces in specialist or leisure magazines. Diaries and journals are supposed to be private documents but many writers use them as practice runs for different kinds of writing or notebooks for reference. Newspaper pieces of the quality of Philip Ochieng or Dominic Odipo's pinpoint and illuminate facts with an elegance that in no way depends on acceptance of the writer's point of view. The Booker prize-winning novelist, Peter Carey, an Australian, cannibalises material. His novel *Oscar and Lucinda*, for example, reproduce long passages from the stunning Victorian autobiography *Father and Son* by Edmund Gosse. It may take a long time to decide whether this puts Carey anywhere near the same rank in literature as Gosse himself. It may raise questions about the law of copyright, which so far protects only a writer's financial interests and those of his heirs up to fifty years after his death. It does not protect the work from later mutilation or misinterpretation, a much harder thing to define. If you look at the existing body of English work considered to be literature, what is sometimes called the *canon*, you will find that Thomas Hobbes' *Leviathan* comes under political science, Robert Burton's *Anatomy of Melancholy* under what we nowadays call psychiatry. Edward Gibbons' *Decline and Fall of the Roman Empire* comes under history, and Thomas Traherne's *Centuries of Meditations* under religion. Yet, because of their magnificent prose style, all of them are read and valued by people who may disagree with the views they express. Other books that are widely known because of their influence on ideas, like Adam Smith's *Wealth of Nations* or Malthus' *Essay on Population,* do not wield the same magic and may be read in paraphrase.

It has been a matter of debate in the last half-century whether there should be a '"canon" at all. The comparison, of course, is with the Christian Bible, where a selection of books made by the early church is regarded as "canonical," essential for all Christians to accept, while others are useful but optional. Other world religions also distinguish between essential scriptures and the commentaries and traditions that are less authoritative. There is obviously a sense in which the list must not become so long that the ordinary reader cannot cover it all, and many later writings are appropriate only to a particular culture or period in history.

One argument in favour of the "canon" is that it provides a reference point, some uniformity between courses taught at different places and times. It is never meant to restrict the areas of reading. Similarly, law students learn the history of specific cases.

In literary matters, where language and technique transform the repetitive content, and where there is no moral requirement for every student to have read everything, the criterion is a bit different in modern times. Not long ago, a student of Latin and Greek "classics" was expected to have read nearly everything in that field, but in modern languages where so much is retained in print, this is not possible. However, some knowledge of the ancient classics is necessary to interpret not only modern European writing like Camus' *Myth of Sisyphus* or James Joyce's *Ulysses* but also the Nigerian writing of Christopher Okigbo or Wole Soyinka. For these, of course, Nigerian history and belief are also fundamental but less fully documented.

Early English literature is not as widely taught as it used to be. This leaves more space for new substantial writers to be added to the canon every few years. It has never been a hard and fast list. The keen students can still select from the old-fashioned series of English classics and find much to give pleasure. What we all have to do is to recognise that there has always been competent writing even if much of this, is not easily accessible to us. Not every book we write can or should repeat what we have already said. Likewise, not all the books we read will be individually remembered. Therefore, there is the process of adding to and subtracting from the public store of impressions all the time. This leaves space for individual enthusiasms and reappraisals.

We sometimes remember a book that influences upon our personal or community circumstances. Kwame Nkrumah's autobiography, *Black Star*, had more impact on popular thought in East Africa in pre-independence times than Achebe's *Things Fall Apart*, which we now see as the literary landmark of the 1950s. J.B Priestley's novel *The Good Companions* is not a great work of art but it gave people in British industrial towns in the hard days of the 1930s a sense of identity. It starts with a football match giving a sense of community to the town. It is hard to recapture that mood nowadays when football matches often bring about violence and controversy. Just after Second World War, French writers and film-makers – Camus, Sartre, Gide, Aragon – set the mood for people puzzled by rapid change in countries that had been less openly divided than France during the years of conflict. For me, Rebecca West's novel *The Fountain Overflows* has given a clue about what it means to be a musician, an experience some of my children have and I do not. Other works are memorable all the time and you can go back to them, as to the Bible, and always find something new. These are books like Dostoevsky's *Crime and Punishment* or Ford Madox Ford's *The Good Soldier*.

It is impossible for the ordinary reader to explore all the work pouring out of the presses. Reviews and critiques help to filter it for us. This has been true for a long time, but much of the work of previous or ancient centuries has vanished. We have either never heard of it or know it from lists and fragments.

Therefore, it would be absurd for you and me to assume that we are likely to add some great and valuable work to the feast of world literature. What we have to do is to delineate, as honestly and tunefully as we can, what little obtrudes itself on our attention. That little will present itself, in the gradual process of erosion and accumulation, within the picture of Kenya, or the Kenyan account of the rest of the world, in the early twenty-first century.

We have classics that are still being read after thousands of years, but not all the works that keep on being reprinted are in the list for their literary quality. H.B. Stowe's *Uncle Tom's Cabin*, A. Dumas' *The Count of Monte Cristo* or D.H. Lawrence's *Lady Chatterley's Lover* are not great literary novels and are not in the "canon." They are markers of certain historical mood or shift of opinion. The names are known even when later works may enlarge and deepen their perspective.

In other arts, as in literature, a classic is a pinnacle of achievement but it is not necessarily the most popular or frequently reproduced piece. A Madonna painted by Raphael in the early sixteenth century is related to the notions of beauty and spirituality accepted in his day as much as to the pigments and canvas available in his day. It does not lose its validity because of a change in those ideals any more than because of a change of materials available. It is going to be supplemented, not replaced, by treatments of the same subject in later generations and in different cultures, but any student of art knows that he is not the first to tackle the subject. What has been written or drawn before is part of the furniture of the mind of the informed writer and reader. If you are not taught to spot these reflections when reading (and much "critical" writing in Kenya stops at the level of thematic analysis and a stereotype of the writer's supposed views) then you can hardly be taught how to incorporate the echoes of larger works into your own small compositions.

I do not recollect any critic relating the whispers/rumour passage in my novel *Coming to Birth* to Virgil or to the echo of Virgil in Beaumarchais. It is not essential to the understanding of the passage to do so, but it is intended to relate our Kenyan experience to community reactions down the ages. I was shocked to have to explain to a university class who Homer was, in respect of a passage they had been given time to prepare. Does a physics class not know the name of Archimedes – or Galileo, Newton or Einstein? Do medical students not get a thrill from Hippocrates, Pasteur, Marie Curie or Christian Barnard? And if, as has been cogently argued, Greek learning was based on Egyptian sources, we have to be prepared to add those earlier names as they are disclosed. The study of literature is a discipline like other academic disciplines. In addition, although it is not essential for every aspiring writer to go through the course, any more than every emergency rescue worker has to be a doctor; each has to share the sensibilities of writers and doctors in the face of human pain, bewilderment and fear.

We live in the twenty first century. We cannot write a thriller that does not take account of the experiences of the last 50 years – decolonisation, the nuclear race, the rise of multinational companies, terrorism and genocide, AIDS and the decline of family values. But when we read stories that predated all these things and still engage our attention – Sol Plaatje's *Mhudi*, Rene Maran's *Batouala*, Kipling's *Kim*, Greene's *The Power and the Glory*, Steinbeck's *Grapes of Wrath* – we know that the writer could not be aware of all these concerns. We must accept the books as they are, expressing, even if criticising, the ideas of their time. Similarly, if we wish to explore the apprehensions of past time, we may have to set aside our notions of hygiene, propriety and labour relations. To enter into the historical imagination of recent writers such as Paul Scott, Ford Madox Ford and William Golding we have to peel away the overlay of contemporary assumptions. We must do it for ourselves: the writer cannot do it for us, but by emphasising certain physical facts more than we do in writing of our own time, the author can *focus* our attention. If you read Ford Madox Ford's *The Fifth Queen* – the lamps and candles flickering in draughty corridors, the rustling of wall hangings, which could easily hide an intruder, the fear of being overheard or misquoted – you enter into the insecurity of a Tudor Court. Ford, writing 350 years after the events, puts his spell on you. But when Shakespeare has Hamlet stab Polonius, "a rat in the arras" (that is, a tapestry woven in the town of Arras) everyone attending the play at that time would know that important people's houses had such wall hangings for warmth as well as decoration, and that they could harbour vermin or eavesdroppers. We do not share the experience of the wall hangings, but we share the sense of fear, the presence of bodyguards and informers. If you read Joseph Heller's *Catch 22* – a great anti-war novel of the twentieth century that has added a catchword to the English language – you will not believe the literal details but you will feel the frustration of servicemen caught up in the war machine.

If I write a novel like *The Present Moment* about the social mobility of Kenyan women in the pre-independence period, it is at one level directed to Kenyans or to comparable African societies: I cannot write out all the assumed knowledge for a reader in Denmark or Australia. He has to accept it as a Kenyan book, giving unfamiliar insights. Moreover, if I read a novel from Denmark, China or Russia, I know it is not directed primarily to me, and my criticism is not based on how much of the story is "relevant" to life in Kenya but on how much it enlarges my view of human experiences and satisfies or provokes my curiosity. Because just as a meal in a gourmet restaurant is wasted on me because I am not interested in the variations of fine food, so a sensitive novel is wasted on you if you only want it to give you ideas, which you can get elsewhere, on increasing your maize yield or running a girls' hostel. You can use novels as resources for sociological or historical research and often get surprising insights from them, but these are subordinate to the subject, themes, characters and images of the story.

The incidental information has nothing to do with the literary rating or the work as long as it is not falsified. An author may often give false information either by being insensitive to human values and limitations or to increase "evidence" for an ideological viewpoint. How often do we read statements like "She opened the wardrobe and selected a dress"? Really? Or, "He was glad to be called up into the army to protect his homeland." Critics may also overlook the audience's saturation point. A new style and setting can create excitement, but it palls as the author or his imitators go on repeating the same formula. Therefore, immediate appraisals of which writers are "important" can change very quickly even at the hands of major critics. Those same critics may be slow to appreciate an enthusiasm that is more social than literary. For instance, the cult of J.R. Tolkien's *Lord of the Rings* pseudo-myths or of A.K. Armah's *Two Thousand Seasons* as against his novels set in modern Ghana. So, it is extremely hard to be objective about contemporary works. Writers who work in multiple forms and subject areas, like Meja Mwangi, Susila Markandaya or Thomas Keneally, may be more challenging models than those who keep mining the same mood and location.

There is something else, which must be said at the risk of causing offence. We are talking about writing in a long literary tradition. For practical purposes, I am evoking examples which are either written in English or accessible in English translation. Since the tradition of writing in English prose Kenya art is only about fifty years old, it is neither comprehensive enough in scope nor distance enough in critical time to constitute the whole referent of a creative writing course.

In his 1998 study, *Urban Obsessions, Urban Fears*, J. Roger Kurtz identifies just over 200 Kenyan novels in English. There have been more since. Many – as in all countries – are easily forgettable. Some (including several of my own) have failed to find publishers. This whole history is only a tiny fraction of the annual output of novels in many countries. Yet, Kenya is, after South Africa, Egypt, and Senegal and in earlier years Nigeria, one of the most sophisticated publishing outlets in Africa. Let us not downplay our own achievement. When Helon Habila, the young Nigerian, winner of the first Caine Prize, came to Kenya for the presentation, the first thing he said to me was, "I have never seen so many people buying books at one time as I saw today in the Text Book Centre."

We should be in a better position if literary works from all over Africa were readily available here in text or translation. These would range from the Latin writings of St. Augustine and other African scholars of the early church, through classical Egyptian writings, Arabic, Ethiopian and Nubian texts, some of them glossed in Greek, as well as nineteenth and twentieth century writings in both indigenous and western languages. *The Women Writing Africa project*, of which the Southern Africa, West Africa and East Africa volumes are already published, gives some idea of the wealth of material available. All book-lovers should be trying to promote the spread of such materials not only in academic libraries but in our private bookshelves and community centres.

Nevertheless, even when this is done, if we aim to reach a mainstream audience and be judged by international standards, we must always be conscious of what is already on the market and what innovation we can make. If you think me harsh, remember that I am a bookseller by trade. Therefore, I know that there is a big catalogue of Swahili books published in Russia and other states of the former Soviet Union. Some are reprints, some translations and others original works. That is a great effort. But, I am sure we should not present them to European students of the Swahili language without reference to the traditional literature of the East African coast. Similarly, writing in English must bear some relation to the tradition of writing in the heartland of English.

We have another heartland in the abundant and continuing oral tradition. All societies have oral traditions, but the boundaries drawn between family or local tradition and the public domain vary from place to place. The modern Luo child may need as much background to explain *Ng'ong'a wuod Odima ma go bunde e wi liech* as the English child needs for King Alfred who burned the cakes (when he took shelter incognito in a village woman's kitchen).

So, just as we have adopted new technologies for ploughing, grinding, transport and political expression, with the appropriate categories and vocabularies, for artistic expression we also need to link on to what the public will accept. A perfect English translation of a folk-tale may fall flat on an audience that has no aversion to the chameleon or the ant-bear. A *nyatiti* player will not bond with his audience through a Cassette Disc (CD). There has to be a long link to make the full impact. Therefore, if you offer Ngugi wa Thiong'o's *A Grain of Wheat* to a class that has never come across a novel before, they may have technical difficulties in dealing with it. It reaches back to a long tradition of discursive story telling. Many of us come to general reading through a first stage of devotion to the Holy Bible or the Holy Koran. The religious aspect of the reading has helped us to persevere, and as a reward, gets a perception of character and narrative that we can carry over into other areas of life.

Cinema is an art with a relatively short history, only a little over a century. Immense changes have occurred – not only the addition of sound and colour to the original black and white images and the expansion of photographic techniques, but also in the very space and address of the film. Much of the admired work of 50 years ago looks unbearably slow to modern viewers. Many modern action films appear crude to connoisseurs. But I don't think anyone could conceive of splitting up that short history by decade or by country. It is all of a piece because it is a visual medium. In writing, language provides boundaries though translation can cross them. Nevertheless, within the language, there has to be continuity.

Looked at it another way, I do not believe that any period of 50 years in English, French or Russian writing would contain enough examples of excellence in all genres to serve as models for teaching creative writing. Even if the period is extraordinarily fertile, that major work will probably require definition and enlargement from outside that time frame. The first half of the 17th century and the first half of the 19th were high points in the literature of England but many major writers overlapped with the periods before and after them and changed accordingly. Meja Mwangi, A.K. Armah and Ama Ata Aidoo are among the African writers who have changed their approach. The millennium is not a cut-off point.

Irish writers have made an enormous contribution to the literature of the British Isles, but this has been so intricately interwoven with other writing in English that it could hardly be regarded as a subject for a separate syllabus.

A singer is expected to perform in a number of different languages. A sculptor uses different techniques to produce work in wood, clay, stone or metal. Although individuals specialise, they expect to learn from fellow-artists. Creators need to respect the rigour of a discipline but they do not discard what alternative methods can bring to light. All this is part of the learning process.

Chapter 3

The Groundwork of the Novel

We have seen that M. Jourdain wanted to improve his way of speaking when he became rich. In Dickens' novel, *Our Mutual Friend,* there is a character that has made a greater leap from rags to riches. Mr. Boffin, who has previously earned a living in the garbage business comes into a fortune on the death of his employer, and one of his desires is to engage someone to read to him. He applies to a street messenger and ballad-singer who he describes as "A literary man – with a wooden leg – and all print is open to him." (Dickens, *Our Mutual Friend*, 93)

> Now it's too late for me to begin shovelling and sifting in alphabets and grammar-books. I'm getting to be an old bird and I want to take it easy. But I want some reading – some fine bold reading, some splendid book in a gorging (gorgeous) Lord Mayor's Show of wollumes (volumes) as'll reach right down to your pint (point) of view, and take time to go by you.   (op. cit, 94)

The storyteller, whether puzzling out the printed word for the illiterate or adding insights and connections to written accounts of everyday things, is doing for his reader something similar to what Silas Wegg does for Mr. Boffin: he is deliberately enriching the other's experience, arousing his emotions and making him think about his situation. "Wegg takes it easy," observes Mr. Boffin, shaken by a reading on Roman history, "I didn't think this morning there was half so many scarers in print. But I'm in for it now." He knows his life has changed once he is open to the written word.

The difference is that the writer cannot take it easy like Mr. Wegg, the intermediary. The author both constructs and participates in the story he tells. Dickens enters into Mr. Boffin's consciousness in terms of "shovelling and sifting", putting the same effort into learning as he previously put into the garbage heap. Dickens' books are among the great novels of English, because he was acquainted with wide variety of characters and their way of expressing themselves in both language and action. The details may be obscure to readers of our times in any part of the world, but we get the sense of vibrant and idiosyncratic characters in a lively society. We can compare these long and intricately plotted stories with the brief evocations of Kenyan moods and voices made by Wahome Mutahi, who could make us, laugh at local differences without malice and bear in mind the serious issues underlying them. If he had been spared for us, we should have looked for more fiction and drama from him. It does not matter that readers in other countries may not recognise terms like *kumikumi* or *Kamukunji*. The context explains them. I was proud to be asked to give an overview of Wahome's works for a journal in Australia.

Therefore, in this chapter, I want to look at some of the basic methods and sources of content in the novel. Some of the novelist's techniques are also useful in the composition of biography and other forms of narrative, such as social history or travel writing. The difference is that fiction can concentrate more on significant themes and images. In real life narrative, these will occur, but always subject to the literal and statistical facts.

We start telling stories when we are very young. Normal families encourage children to talk about their experiences and impressions. Conversation is the great East African art form and many of the ideas for my stories have been picked up from talk overheard in buses and *matatus* (informal public transport vans). Creativity is not limited to what is put down on paper. Those of us who love reading may feel the urge to catch the story and set it out in permanent form. This may just be because it is a good story or because we see a lesson for practical living in it, or because it gives us a clue to understanding behaviour and events that puzzle us, or because the events of the story symbolise our understanding of life and death, duty or morality. But if we choose to put our reflections in story form, rather than in journalism or textbooks, then the result has to *be* a story. The events and characters relate to one another in some meaningful way. The reader at the end of the book understands the time and place even if not at the beginning.

To say, "I went to school. I had *ugali* and *sukuma* for lunch. I did my homework. I went to bed," is not a story. It is not even a diary entry. You will only put this in a novel if you want to portray tedium and the sameness of day-to-day events. Stories tell us something out of the ordinary. They have to have a plot to move the characters from the opening situation to the closing one and to draw the threads together. An investigative journalist, just like a detective novelist, shows us how movements in the bank account of *A* relate to threats against *B* and the suspicious disappearance of *C*. Each of the three separate events does not constitute a story. There has to be a demonstrable relation between them. Therefore, the novelist must be consistent about the ages and characteristics of the protagonists and the situations which brought them together.

We have all read the sort of story that says, "She decided to leave for Paris in the morning." But unless she has already been shown to be a traveller with plenty of money and no ties, she doesn't just make such a decision. She has to have a passport and a visa, money for the ticket and a source of foreign exchange. She will need time off from work and if she is sharing a house with someone, she must make domestic arrangements. The author does not necessarily have to explain all this, but if she expects to be believed, she must demonstrate the possibility. Perhaps the character is on leave and house warming for a friend, so she is not in a regular routine, which the neighbours are used to. She has some prize money to spend, and her passport is still valid since she returned from a course overseas. But if she just decamps from home and job, she will be aware that people will be searching for her, and that too could be part of the story. In real life, most of us can tell the difference between an acquaintance pitching us a yarn in an attempt to borrow money and someone genuinely describing what happened to her. When you are learning a new procedure, whether it is playing a game, baking a cake or offering your imaginative work to the public, it is good to get used to the basic rules before attempting variations.

Of course, odd things often happen in real life. Someone starts getting children in middle age. Cousins meet in a distant place without knowing they are related. Someone wins money in a sweepstake. A glamorous career follows a talent competition. We talk about these things, and the conversation may be the germ of a story. But we do not take the events for granted. They have to be accounted for.

In Emily Bronte's *Wuthering Heights* or Cormac McCarthy's *The Orchard Keeper,* we are not given an account of the years during which a wild teenager leaves the scene and comes back as a moneyed man. But we do know something about how other people reacted to the event and how that period of absence affects the rest of the story. In real life, a person called up for war service often has experiences, which he can hardly communicate to his family at home, but they are aware of signs of change in him.

People who need to keep their movements secret—criminals, spies, detectives—need more than anyone else to be able to give an alleged reason for being where they are. I would like someone to try to write a story in which the conventions of a spy thriller operate in East Africa—the call that has to be made at exactly 8.12 from the middle call box outside the Post Office, the letter that will give instructions for procedures next morning, the other half of a torn-off postcard that identifies the messenger. Surely, the call box will be occupied or out of order; the letter will be in the pocket of a security guard who dares not leave it lying about, the first half of the postcard will have been thrown away by the housemaid. A street child will be sleeping in the barrow which was to have served as a dead letter drop, and the door for which a duplicate key has been provided will have been heavily padlocked by auctioneers. Our plots must allow for ordinary life going on round the characters.

One of the techniques of dealing with improbability in a story is to start with the move so that the gaps in our knowledge are filled in retrospectively as the SMSs are recorded and the overdrawn and overstayed threats start coming in.

At the same time, a story is a story. It has to show how time goes on, how people change, sometimes how dull life is while they are waiting for a letter from an absent friend, an appointment or an election result. So, we should not overload the plot by making every simple event carry the burden of being symbolic. A life where every item has special significance is not easy to believe in.

What, then, sets the writer off exploring a situation and a set of characters? It may be a long-time interest, a memory, an unexplained event or a revelation. The great Russian writer Dostoevsky was a fast and fluent worker. He was a compulsive gambler and often had to write for money to repay his debts. But we read that before writing *The Idiot,* he was greatly moved by Holbein's picture of taking Christ down from the Cross, which he saw in Geneva, and made eight different versions of the first draft of the story. (Magarshack: Introduction to *The Ediot*). He then wrote part one rapidly but each of the other parts caused him great agony and many changes of mind. If this can happen to a great novelist, how much more can it happen to you and me. Creative work is of necessity, making a choice among alternatives. It must not be hurried and it must not exclude the possibility of a change of mind. The Bible tells us that the potter can mould the same clay time after time till it comes out right. The creative instinct is to know when it is right.

When you write a story or tell one orally, you present a setting shared by the teller or the tale and the reader. If it is *fable* – much oral literature consists of fable – the background is not usually very detailed. It keeps to the simple facts of life in almost any society. If you relate the fable to a more sophisticated background, as Rebeka Njau does in *The Sacred Seed*, you bring it nearer to the novel, because each character has more choices to make. George Orwell's *Animal Farm*, which we have in Swahili as *Shamba la Wanyama*, is close to a fable. The farm is not set in a particular place or time, and it is the animals that enact the satire on political society. This is very different from his novel *1984* where possible horrors of a totalitarian state are described in a specifically English setting.

An allegory may have a more detailed setting than a fable, but all these details are made to have moral or religious meaning connected with each aspect of the literal meaning. St. Paul's passage in *Ephesians* about putting on the whole armour of God is constructed in this way. Each piece of military equipment is given a parallel spiritual quality. *The Pilgrim's Progress* by John Bunyan is one of the most famous book-length allegories and for that reason has been translated into many languages. Bunyan was what we would now call a *jua kali* mechanic: he worked at making odd items serviceable. So, he was able to find a concrete term for abstract ideas that helped the reader make sense of them.

Making sense is not necessarily commanding credence. Are all stories meant to be convincing? Events in real life are often inconclusive. Now in fairy tales and folklore, which are the first stories most of us learn to recognise, the end is frequently not believable in the terms proposed by the rest of the story. Seven beautiful girls emerge from the frog's stomach no-one has told us he is not an ordinary-sized frog. A person is turned to stone. A voice emerges from inside an animal that has eaten someone. A goose lays golden eggs. Vegetables stored in a pot turn into a live baby (What might have happened if you tried to cook half of them?) These things can only be believed if you turn the naturalistic beginnings of the story upside down.

Scholars will give you all kinds of complicated theories about their psychological significance and technical skill. The plain fact is that we often invent or accept stories because we wish things were not as they are or because we think putting something into words will give us power over it. This is like claiming to have borne a miracle baby in three months. It is a strong element of fiction and accounts for the kind of novel where the couple lives happily ever after the wedding or the James Bond type hero escapes against impossible odds. Writing or reading such a story may give harmless relief from real world problems.

There is another kind of fantasy story like Thomas Pynchon's *Gravity's Rainbow*, Ben Okri's *The Famished Road* or J.M. Coetzee's *Life and Times of Michael K*. We are not meant to believe them in a literal sense and yet they give a vivid sense of reality. Some incidents are larger than life but they are not falsified. Disbelief is partially suspended. In some ways, they are like those trick photographs which enormously exaggerate the size of a human hair or a speck of sugar so that you cannot guess what it is but are led to believe what you are told rather than what you see. This is not the same as magic realism, which superimposes on the literal background of a place – what people eat, what work they do, what streets they walk through –another level of action with a fairytale quality that is not in the time dimension of hard fact. In *Midnight's Children* by Salmon Rushdie, where a psychic link is alleged to exist among the children born close to the minute of India's independence, this does not prevent the reader understanding the chronological account of the children's separate lives. Gabriel Marquez's *One Hundred Years of Solitude* leaves us with the impression that after so many revolutions most things remain the same. *The Last Harmattan of Alisoune Dunbar* is an African example by Syl Cheney-Coker.

There is a distinction between possibility, probability and plausibility. The facts asserted have to be possible *in terms of the thought world of the story*. If the princess can sleep for a hundred years, then the beast can also turn into a man. If soldiers in the Great War can drown in the mud of the battlefields, we can understand that some deliberately injure themselves to get away from the fighting. If the ragman can become a millionaire, some millionaires must release the funds by falling upon had bad times. The possible events do not have to be probable, since life is full of impossibilities, but it helps the reader along if some of them are.

To be plausible, arguable, is something very different. In Grace Ogot's story "The White Veil" it is hardly possible to believe that Achola does not recognise the figure and voice of the girl he was previously engaged to, or that the priest will hold her vow, under a false name, binding.

In *Our Mutual Friend*, where Silas Wegg reads to Mr. Boffin, there are many improbabilities, which we swallow for the sake of the story. But when it is alleged that Mr. Boffin has had a change of character and become grasping and ill tempered, urging Bella to make a rich marriage, this is beyond belief. Boffin has been built up as a humane and generous character, eager to foster the romance between Bella and John while they do not know that John has a rich heritage. Dickens explains this as a trick to test their reactions. We do not believe Mr Boffin could be party to such a trick. It is a fault in Dickens' work and would be a disaster if perpetrated by a more modest talent. The writer has lost his reader as soon as the magic hold over his imagination is released. This may not always be the author's fault. The reader may be so attached to expectations of a happy ending, or of one that conforms to his personal sense of justice, that he blames the story rather than his own partiality. For instance, some readers dislike Meja Mwangi's *Carcase for Hounds* because the wounded general is portrayed as a failure. But it is a fact of life that in all campaigns, there are successes and failures on both sides, and it would be unrealistic to suppose otherwise. The writer's aim is not to transform history but to share his insights with the reader.

Usually, the teller of the realistic novel has thorough knowledge of the background. He may tickle the reader's fancy by introducing local details appreciated only by a few, like old-fashioned names of real places or technical details of craftsmanship. But he must beware of readers more knowledgeable in a particular area. When John le Carre wrote *The Constant Gardener*, with a lot of the action set in Kenya, he learned a tremendous amount about *matatus*, Kibera, Kenyatta Hospital and a lot of it came out exactly right. But he did not understand the Kenyan obsession with corpses or the paperwork that is involved in a hospital releasing a dead or live baby. That does not prevent its being a very fine novel. Not only does he write almost faultless prose in all his works, but also he is a master of the cinema-style "cut" from one scene to another which is required in fast-paced modern writing. Dickens and his contemporaries were helped in these transitions by the fact that their work often came out in instalments in magazines. Nonetheless, the instalments, where they are marked in modern editions, usually included more than one strand in the story. But they had an unhurried audience and could write in linking paragraphs. TV watchers and mobile phone users expect instant connection to the new scene. That is just a warning to immerse yourself thoroughly in the society you are describing.

Several of my stories bring in small financial misdeeds or inconclusive negotiations that go on all the time, but I would not possibly, be capable of describing the Goldenberg scale of operations[1]. You can refer to this as a public event, or as something

---

[1]   Goldenberg refers to a financial/political scandal in Daniel arap Moi's government involving millions of shillings looted from Kenyan Treasury

that affects one of your characters because a company reduces staff on account of it, or because a girl attending the hearings meets a friend there. But an account of the inside workings needs special knowledge. Richard Cox is a banker who wrote a book about Kenya some thirty years ago and went on after he had left to write some fascinating financial thrillers that appear to be totally authentic. Those I have read are not set in Kenya but show general acquaintance with Eastern Africa. In novel-writing, as in any other job, we have to start from what we absolutely know and venture slowly into exploring new areas and keeping up to date. My novel *Victoria* was written in Tanzania in the 1970s and the events had to be set in Kenya in the 1960s so as to link up with *Murder in Majengo*. But I did not even think of publishing it until I had come back to live in Kenya and authenticate the descriptions.

Children can often accept statements which an adult would have doubts about because they are learning new and improbable things all the time. But when the story comes back from the realm of ogres and spiders to the home village, they will ask more searching questions. So we may, even as adults, agree that the romantic hero or heroine has unlimited riches, but we still expect that the tickets will be paid for and the luggage looked after.

Some critics may make you think that it is "better" to write about Africans than about Chinese people, about farmers than about factory workers, but in the end, what matters is the writer's understanding and the readers' sympathy. Most often, we like reading about something unfamiliar. A story set in another country or among wealthy people in circles that we do not often penetrate requires the author to set the scene in detail. It is permissible to invent a completely new setting, as in science fiction, which is good exercise in consistency. What in my view an author must NOT do is to falsify a real place or time. You can invent a nameless

---

through subsidy of exports of gold far beyond standard arrangements during the 1990s.

space compatible with the action of your story. Alternatively, in the mode of magical realism, you can relate what happens at a given place and time to experiences of similar characters at the same place at another time. In real life, similarly, a visit to a historic site or a place of worship may make us conscious of the memories and prayers enshrined there.

I do not undervalue the spiritual or symbolic content of stories. Authors as different as A.K. Armah, Thomas Hardy, James Joyce, E.L. Doctorow, Wole Soyinka and Charles Williams use myth and inherited ritual in their own way. But religious experience is for most of us deeply embedded in everyday life. It is never vague. The rules of consistency and of narrative authenticity, multifarious as they are, still apply.

There are differences of pace and perspective emphasised in the post-modernist period though not entirely new. Anyone can experiment with them, just as the remake of a classic film often amounts to a speeding-up of the action. This is quite different from moving events to an incompatible time or register, setting a slapstick comedy into a tragic frame or imposing political ideas on to a time that had not yet heard of them.

In *The English Patient,* the bomb disposal routines ring true even in an exaggerated sense, but the events at the villa could not have happened in the war-torn Italy of 1945. The beauty of Ondaatje's prose writing cannot blind us to that. Young army nurses are not allowed to live out of camp and care alone for politically valuable patients. Blown spies are not given access to sources of intelligence. Petrol is not available for unauthorised travel in wartime. Villagers will not keep their hands off linen and medicines they need for their own partisan casualties and deserters.

Some post-modernist critics say that, because we do not know all about the past, we are entitled to play about with it. That is not generally true. We can know a good deal about the past, perhaps more than about the present, where people are busy hiding things.

We know the story, once top secret, of the Enigma Machine processing wartime intelligence at Bletchley Park, but we do not yet know who set up the stories about the "Millennium Bug" that was thought to endanger our computers on 1 January 2000, or what they cost. We cannot tell the audience *all* about society unless we are tremendously able people writing very detailed works like those of Dickens and Tolstoy. Even if we were, our readers and publishers can seldom afford to give us that much scope.

So, if our characters are confined to a small segment of the scene – parents of children in private schools or shop workers or long distance hauliers – we will show how things look to their eyes and so reflect a little of the wider community and possibly, the author's view of it. The fact that they may not be active on the public scene does not make them peripheral. Each of us is central in our sphere of life.

The point of view of the character can be different from that of the author. The reader must always be sensitive to who is making an observation and what it tells about the character portrayed. It would hardly be possible to write a story in which all the participants are "politically correct," and if it were, it could not be an interesting story. The storyteller has to do his researches and then exercise his imagination. No theory of how things ought to have been can make up for failure to perceive how things actually were.

The Australian Nobel Prize winner Patrick White says, "All the houses I have lived in have been renovated and refurbished to accommodate fictions," (*Flaws in the Glass*, 156). The language will be couched in the writer's own style, but it may be possible to catch the flavour of the period by quoting some contemporary writing and imitating it. Such pastiche is difficult to do well. One can underline period change by pointing out developments in certain words, for instance, that "nice" originally meant "discriminating" and that "silly" meant "innocent" or "naïve."

Possibly, you will have to explain to your children what "foolscap", "transparent" and "chill" meant.

A biographer needs to fill in some background events, and may restrict what he has to say about the domestic life of the subjects. The novelist will refer to public events either as the characters apprehend them or as they are unknowingly affected by them. Changes in taxation, for instance, and crop prices are known to the small farmer, even if he does not see them set out in the newspaper. The novelist, drawing out of a story such reflections on life and morality, is interested first in what his characters perceive but also in what determines events. The Joad family, for instance, in John Steinback's *The Grapes of Wrath*, do not realise that their own poor farming practices have helped turn Oklahoma into dustbowl, or that their own refugee presence is upsetting the economy of other states. It is their determination to stay alive and humane that makes the story. But the reader is acutely aware of the larger issues. Critics sometimes dismiss Jane Austen's novels, written by the unmarried daughter of a clergyman at the very beginning of the nineteenth century, because of their narrow scope and middle class outlook. Indeed, the author had to write what she knew, and makes fun of the sensational "Gothic" romances written by some of her contemporaries like Mrs. Ann Radcliffe. But she was not – women generally are not – as sheltered as theorists like to pretend. Her brothers became very senior naval officers, and she shows knowledge of how sailors could augment their income by capturing a prize ship. She knows what goes on in the sordid "sponging houses" where people were imprisoned for debt. She could never have set foot in one, but she understands the circumstances. There are times when all of us are well advised not to go into details about a scene we have not seen at first hand, but stick to plain facts. Jane Austen had found it difficult to reject a proposal of marriage from an Irish soldier: this may have been the source of her sister Kitty Bennett's running away with a soldier, to the horror of her family. She knew a great deal about class distinctions, though not the extremes of wealth and poverty, and when one of her heroines, a seventeen-year-old girl, has to make a difficult journey by stagecoach without an escort, the mother accepts the fact that she has acted sensibly. She is annoyed that the host family has been so inconsiderate, but not unduly distressed.

So, a story can broaden out from an apparently narrow focus to tell us a good deal about society. In *From a Crooked Rib,* Farah uses the perceptions of a nomadic girl who thinks a cluster of ten houses is a town to recreate for us urban and rural life in Somalia.

If you are depicting a real scene, whether in a novel or a history book, and it is outside your own experience, you must make every effort to recreate the facts by reading, visiting places, talking with people who have similar experiences: even if the mechanics of the experience is different – visiting the Arctic Circle and seeing the midnight sun in a modern cruise ship is not like going there in a wooden boat under sail – the actual sights, sounds and emotions will be in some ways similar. Even if you go to Hell's Gate National Park in a Pajero, you will still feel you are seeing the world on creation day. You will study photographs and paintings of the time. You will certainly not use in the story all the material you uncover – I well know the temptation of wanting to put everything in – but you internalise so that your mind is in tune with it. Notice the names given to people – a foreigner may not attach significance to being called Gladwell, Jacinta, Benta, Fanis, Murray or Willis, but we Kenyans do. If you cannot find an actual model of a room in Kisumu in 1938, ask yourself, "what is the floor like? Are there windows? Is there artificial lighting? What kind of furnishing? Who comes in and out? Were the materials you imagine available at that time and place? Is there a radio? If so, it will be housed in a big box. Do people ring a bell or knock at a door? What language is being spoken? Does everyone understand it? How do they address one another?"

Writing a novel is very much like having a baby. You should never do it unless you are prepared to devote years of your life to it. There is a positive beginning, whether or not we can exactly date it, and there is a time appointed for severance: a few incidental events may alter that expected date of delivery (a state of health, a personal or public event that compels a break) but the process has its own momentum. The length of the pregnancy is determined by the nature of the conception. Any nugget of information relating to a character or event we are embodying is picked up and sucked for nourishment as eagerly as those special brown or white stones expectant mothers can buy in the market for minerals supply in their bodies.

This is why I have given separate sections to plots, themes and narrative and not to character. The characters are there from the beginning; often certain incidents occur only because of the temperament and interests of the people involved in them, not the other way round. Plot and theme do not develop without people, and people are all around us. Our ideas of character are derived from experience and observation. We can invent a story but I do not believe we ever really invent a person. Like an actor learning a part in a play, we study how the named person will walk, talk, eat and arrange his business. These things are normal to him whether the plot we have designed round him takes place or not. Of course, the events we set up may change him in some ways. Mr. Boffin did not have much time for listening to history when he was still raking over the garbage heap. Meja Mwangi's Frank Fundi would not have been promoting the sale of condoms if he had been allowed to complete his veterinary studies overseas. But what the writer has to learn is primarily to choose the right word to describe the person and record his speech. I do not believe that anyone who is not genuinely interested in people can write fiction successfully.

Anthony Burgess, an accomplished novelist and critic says, "I have to do it: there are half-invented people and half-conceived actions in my brain, and they have to be completed and released into novels for the sake of my own comfort"(*The Novel Now, 210*). This is true. The characters, like the baby, struggle to get out and separate themselves when they are ready. We cannot safely hurry them, and we cannot dismiss them.

In the same book, Burgess praises the fine novelist Henry Green for a less common quality that he can achieve in prose "that unity, close-knit and taut, we find in the sonnet form. His novels stay in our minds as entities" (Burgess). All too often, we remember good novels by certain episodes or characters: there is something special in remembering one for the whole area of society it represents.

A story consists of words on the page, or in the reader's or writer's memory. With the last word the story stops. Beyond that, what happens to the characters is their own affair. They are out of our control as much as the person we once conversed with on a long bus journey and never see again. It is frivolous to create a "biography" of a character that goes outside the framework of the given story.

It is often expected that a novel will address the general public, but sampling will show that there is usually some restriction implied. What seems to the "us" of the writer an obvious, difficult, wise, foolish or ridiculous action has a lot to do with our class, community or religion.

Writing can be communally closed. Ngugi Wa Thiong'o's early work relates to what touches on the Kikuyu world only. This does not mean that outside readers may not react with empathy, but that some issues are closed out. *Petals of Blood* shows a broadening of scope. Each of the types has its justification. Few villages are neatly self-contained but a far-away reader may understand an isolated village better than a sprawling, amorphous new township. We may see what the villagers have in common rather than the private relationships which keep them in some ways apart. What is not permissible is to depict a part and claim it to be the whole.

Much British and American writing is nationally closed. The unit of potential readership is so large that until recent migrations, the writer might not have needed to envisage an outside audience. But within the nation, it may also be communally closed in a sense of class or locality. To the ordinary English reader from a working family, the novels of Iris Murdoch are essentially foreign, a lot of clever talk from people who don't have to get up in the morning. The hand to mouth existence depicted in Akare's *The Slums* will shock some of the prudent families housed in Pumwani or Eastleigh. A greater writer like Henry Green separates the microcosms for the sake of brevity and still communicates between them. It took a great publishing imagination to combine his contrasting novels, *Living, Loving and Party-Going* in one volume.

This is a significant example. Green was the son of a rich manufacturer who required him to learn the trade from the factory floor. He therefore had actual experience of life at different economic levels and areas of choice. George Orwell had to experiment deliberately to immerse himself in these extremes, though he was never free of real life financial anxieties. For each story, the author has to select a boundary and a target in order to make a significant statement and search out what Ngugi calls "a fiction language." The story is not going to solve problems in society: it may expose and analyse problems in such a way that individuals, religious leaders and government get an insight into what options they have. So the choice of area defines rather than restricts. Paul Scott writes about the Raj, the British presence in India. He gives convincing and sympathetic portraits of many Indian characters, but no one writer can portray the enormous spectrum of India. These characters are depicted in relation to the final years of the Raj and the families – military, administrative, missionary and business-oriented (like Tusker and Lucy after independence) – affected by public events. Just as the European presence in Kenya was never monolithic but included great differences in class, taste, speech and standard of living, even more in India, where many white families had made their home over four or more generations, there was great diversity.

Writing can be communally closed but extended by explanation, as when Grace Ogot in *The Strange Bride* says, "Owiny left and went to his *samba* (a young man's cottage in his father's home). The interpretation is more skilful when it falls within the action: this is one of Achebe's great strengths. But most of us need to explain words from time to time. Akare's distinction in *The Slums* between Ofafa Maringo and Ofafa Kunguni is not significant to a reader who knows no Swahili.

Some writing is really class or communally neutral. For instance, in *Three Days on the Cross,* Wahome Mutahi deliberately uses non-Kenyan surnames and suppresses the local idioms identified with his newspaper column. He sacrifices intimacy to make a general point. We all have areas of concern where our personal bias shows even though the story indicates that many fail in this respect. These are areas where a person of conscience cannot pretend to be neutral.

We may have a copy of a treaty or a deed of sale to assert the objective existence of an event that has moved us, but no records of the negotiations or inducements by which it was thrashed out, the smells and traffic noises of the scene. William Styron's magnificent novel about the Nat Turner slave rebellion of 1831 in Virginia is based on very thorough research. But by filling out certain conversations and incidents, it indicated what the character would know or could not know at that place and time. We see Nat reading out a signpost to his illiterate white captors, and see the moment when he first hears himself described as a slave though he has been brought up as a member of his master's family. We grasp the impossibility of the slave-holder freeing him easily. Certain legal forms have to be complied with to prevent the freed man being seized by someone else, probably a harsher master. The novel makes us physically present in the way a documentary history, blank to people's tone of voice, forms of address, their dress and the places they could acceptably meet, could never do.

The novelist does not claim what he writes to be literally true, only notionally true within the limits he has defined for himself. He can dress characters in blue or green as suits him, but he must not assert a limit and then break with it. Only for an explicit and compelling reason, will his characters act against the conventions of their place and time, or show surprise at them.

The accumulated background information must never take precedence over our more intimate understanding of the accidents and oddities of human behaviour. Completely, ordinary people do not inspire us to write about them. Men and women around us do not always behave according to strict law and custom, nor do natural and public events always conform to a prescribed pattern. People in private do not stick to an officially acceptable vocabulary, and they do not always know the things a historian expects them to know. Governments often keep military movements, and the reasons for them, secret from common people. What is more, the implications of an event may not be clear at the time. For example, the population of monitor lizards in Nyanza has drastically reduced because the revised 8-4-4 music syllabus led thousands of schoolchildren to catch them in order to make *orutu* (a one-string instrument). Previously, only those with special musical gifts had tried to make and play the instrument. On a world scale, the people of Nagasaki, victims of the second atomic bomb in 1945, did not know that a bomb had been dropped on Hiroshima a few days before, though they had heard rumours of a new weapon. The doctors treating "radiation sickness" did not know about its genetic effects, not because of a news blackout but because it had never occurred before.

Everyone in my generation knows – most of those reading this book know, though less obsessively – that a puff of smoke indoors indicates a person smoking tobacco. But most likely, these readers' grandchildren will not know it at all. But unfashionable people, other than a few sailors, in late sixteenth century Europe, did not know it, and wondered why a seaman or an explorer back from

America should be setting himself on fire. Many jokes were made about that. That is what the novelist has to be conscious of, since it is not something statistically recorded, and this is what will make the reader feel he is actually in Tudor England.

Characters are distinguished by their speech as depicted by words on the page: there is diction appropriate to each and these interact in the reader's ear. So, we have to be conscious of the pitfalls in writing dialogue.

Most of the time, we talk in incomplete sentences with pauses and abbreviations. Few people make set speeches. So, you have to find a middle way to represent the sense of a conversation making up in words for the looks and gestures we understand when we are talking to somebody face to face. When we are translating, for instance, representing Luo conversation in English, it is not correct to translate word for word, so that the speaker is represented as being unfamiliar with the structure of the language, or to use the sort of English the speaker would use if he were talking in that language: to do so is to misrepresent the situation. Most Luo speakers use words correctly and idiomatically and we want to present them in the narrative as speaking in that same register. Generally, their mode of speaking is not part of the subject. It is only a small child or a foreigner who will be represented as making mistakes in speech. If different dialects are being used, it is generally best just to say so. To introduce variant English dialects is only confusing: I have seen translations from the French which are very misleading in this way. So, when a gifted writer like Achebe flavours his prose by bringing in proverbs or catch phrases from the language represented, this is an extra wealth. They are always translated into correct English in the style of address appropriate to the fictional speaker. We can do the same with English sayings like "after the Lord Mayor's Show comes the dust cart" or "a nod is as good as a wink to the blind horse," and make sure that the sense is conveyed within the passage instead of having to be the subject of separate note.

But sometimes, the characters' failure to understand one another is the point of the story. It may be a doctor explaining to a patient what is wrong with him in such complex terms that the ordinary person is baffled, or it may be someone talking in pidgin English or Sheng in a way familiar only to certain age groups or classes. Then the reader has sympathy with the character who does not understand. This technique is used also in film.

Also as in film, there will be details that some of the audience miss. Just as a teacher knows that not every point he makes will be grasped by everyone in the class, so the writer knows that some subtleties of language, custom or social difference will not be understood by all readers. This is not a reason to leave them out. In both cases, you have, without looking down on anybody, to say as much as you can and try to see that the main themes of the story are clear in terms that most readers will follow. You must never despise your audience or appraise their intelligence in terms of your own special studies.

When reading a novel about horse racing, ballet or nuclear research most of us have to accept the author's technical vocabulary. Similarly, the jockey, the dancer and the physicist are not bound to know our terminology relating to age sets, customary avoidances or food preparation in East Africa. That does not mean we cannot reach them in many ways and stimulate their curiosity.

But the proverb says that even Homer, the greatest poet, sometimes nodded and let his attention slip. We do not make a song and dance about it every time mother makes the tea or prepares water for hand washing. So, normally intelligent readers will also come to take it for granted that in Achebe's world, the kola nut is broken and the chalk rolled across the floor, for specific occasions.

Chapter 4

Themes

Serious fiction writing generally has a theme as well as a story. There is no generalisation that does not allow for exceptions. You may find that an adventure story like *Treasure Island* by Robert L. Stevenson or a funny story like *Hekaya za Abunuwasi na Hadithi Nyingine* is so absorbing that it need not be referred back to mything outside itself. Critics sometimes complicate our lives unnecessarily by alleging layers of meaning that the text cannot bear. This does not mean that having a gripping and complex story is not important or that detective stories and romances are to be written off as only what some call "popular," not worth analysis. The great work of Graham Greene in the middle years of the 20th century was to demonstrate that a well-written thriller can attract an audience and at the same time, deal with the religious and ethical problems of the time. He divided his works into those called novels and those called entertainments, but all are written with the same skills and elegance. His effect on others may have been more important than any of his individual books, but readers in Kenya can still enjoy reading *The Power and the Glory* or *Brighton Rock*, which illustrates some of the ways in which England of the 1930s is like Kenya in the 2000s, where you can call still win a prize by asking for a *Farmer's Choice* sausage. If Greene had never written, the novels of Albert Camus, John le Carre, Alex la Guma and Meja Mwangi might be different from those we know.

I do not personally think it matters very much, whether the story comes first and theme emerges or whether the theme presents itself and then one looks for a story to exemplify it. For instance, when I was writing *Coming to Birth,* the actual story of a Luo girl brought to the mission house by a white policeman had never left my mind. I characterised the girl under the name Paulina. What happened to her and her consciousness of public events parallels the growth of the Kenya nation. The incident came first, the theme of political awareness followed.

Homing In, was written to answer the question why old white ladies, who have had very little to do with African life for many years, identify themselves persistently with Kenya and refuse to leave when they are aged and alone. The first thing Ellen (one of the characters) learns from Kenya is to go back to work and send her children to boarding school. Not surprisingly, she loses Angela and is distanced from Nigel. Her way of life is shocking to her mother and sisters. How could she settle comfortably in England where the nurture of children is of supreme importance?

Theme and story are intimately connected in the mind, so it does not matter which comes first. The work of writing the book is to recognise and verbalise the connections. The greatest of recent Kenyan novels, *The Last Plague* by Meja Mwangi, is obsessed with the theme of AIDS and how to control its spread. The author rarely talks about the way he works, but it seems to me obvious that he looked about for a way to express this and came up with the marvellously economical scenario of a tea-room and a small business located at a cross-roads away from the main modern highway and basically five characters – one of whom is off-stage most of the time – revolutionising the situation in a way that is comic and tragic and socially effective all at once.

Having put these two elements together, Meja Mwangi then employs his magical verbal gift to give a distinct idiom to each speaker and to carry the reader along with the repetitive marker of the theme: "where there is one (grave) there will be two, where there are two there will be four, where there will be four there will be eight...." Because the book is so single-minded, the process can clearly be studied. My own book *Chira*, which I thought (mistakenly), would be my last novel, had to carry all the things I had left to say, and so it combines the AIDS theme with others, particularly with the religious thought-world of a young Luo man living in the city. How did it come about? Certainly, I knew there had to be a serious study of AIDS. But our failure to face squarely the medical and social facts of the pandemic arises from self-contradictory views of moral commitment, of cause and effect and of telling the truth. So, what story will contain these? The story of the relationship between a young man living in town and his rural family, between religious belief and *juok*, between power and pretence? Little by little, the characters impose their own logic on the scene.

Chancing to see two young men greeting one another on the City Square flyover helped me to actualise them. Some details – the visiting football team seeking assistance from a *mganga* (medicine man) for instance, – come from real life. When I had finished the story and was carrying a copy for the first time to the publisher for consideration, I passed a hair salon – maybe a little more sophisticated than the one I had pictured in Huruma – and there were three smartly dressed young men clustered round the door, just like the scene in the book. I do not know what they were doing there since I hurried on to catch my *matatu*. This is an example of the coincidences that give the writer confidence in having seen it right.

Paul Scott, who will, I believe, in time come to be seen as one of the finest twentieth century novelists, gives an extraordinarily detailed account of the process of writing a novel called *The Birds of Paradise* in a talk given in 1961 and called "Imagination in the Novel" (Scott, *My Appointment with the Muse*). The starting-off point is a picture that came to his mind of a mature woman appearing in a doorway and leaving the impression that something had come to an end. He tried to fit this into a novel he had planned to write about Spain, but it did not work out. In due course, however, the woman's name becomes Dora who is associated with a man called Bill and with something that glitters. The glittering resolves itself into beautiful birds of paradise. These are found in the islands off New Guinea, but their exotic plumes were used in the headgear of Indian princes, who may also have kept stuffed specimens for display. Scott now conceives the doorway as the door of a cage in which the dead birds were housed, where the man and woman were revisiting a scene of their youth. The cage is also an image of the diminishment of the princes in the new Dominion of India. From that time on, Scott's work was to concentrate on interconnected novels portraying the last years of the British Raj (empire) in India.

Having reached that point in constructing the novel, Scott says (ibid. 19f):

> Imagination is not enough. Knowledge is necessary. And experience of the oddity of life. The imagination, the knowing and the experience finally cohere into a pattern... And in one sense, the work of the larger imagination is finished. ... producing characters who are needed but who tend, through the imagination, to change the totality of the book by their own strong demands.

That puts it in a nutshell; so the opening words of the story are not the beginning of the invention but the beginning of the transmission to the reader of the concept the writer has already rounded out, disregarding false starts in Spain or elsewhere.

In an even more detailed account of the writing of his more complex book *The Jewel in the Crown*, Scott quotes the first paragraph of the novel and says, "It was not the first paragraph written. Between the originating image and the pinning it down on the page, there is often a terrible gap of time and changing circumstance. If it is a good hard image, it will stand. Nothing will erode it. But it is extremely difficult to co-ordinate it with all the succession of images it gives birth to" (*My Appointment with the Muse,* 60).

Paul Scott is a master of his craft whom I greatly revere. I cannot doubt that he is telling the truth about how he works and how some other great novelists work. But, in literature as in our daily human relationship, we must avoid the temptation to generalise or to twist words into a meaning they do not have for everybody. It is good to start cautiously and admit that not all of us co-ordinate all the images all the time.

In an article on the Chilean poet and Nobel Prize winner, Pablo Neruda, Charles Simic, the fine American poet, says that in magical realism, there is a rejection of any distinction between the magical and the real.

It is true that the two elements are mixed or alternated in a story or poem using this mode, but the very fact we recognise and name them shows that they are not identical. This is not to deny that the author may accord them equal weight; the sizing up of major and minor elements will be different in every work. But the writer knows what he is doing. We may be dazzled by the interplay among the children born at the moment of India's independence in Rushdie's *Midnight's Children* but we are not really fooled. If we were, we should not appreciate the artistry of the invention. *Invention* is coming upon, finding something that has not been known before and putting it in use. It is one of the oldest terms in literary criticism. Invention follows *discovery*. People *discovered* electricity, which is a natural force, and then went on to *invent* the power generator.

So, a writer discovers, opens up, for example, an old hidden path through the forest. She is inspired – gets a fresh breath of air – by the notion that this has historical significance, and goes on to invent a story in which a group of people used this path to get from one historical situation to another. The result may be a novel. Think of how many children's stories, in particular, are associated with secret pathways, escape routes and underground passages. It is the readers who will collectively decide whether it works, whether it is believable. If it does not command belief, at least for the duration of the reading, it does not work as a novel, however fine its craftsmanship may be. R.L. Stevenson's *Dr. Jekyll and Mr. Hyde*, a book about dual personality, famous as it is, never convinces me. The same author's *Treasure Island*, perhaps because it is written for young readers, holds most of us spellbound. *Spellbound* is the operative word. The writer's magic kit is his gift with words, and at best, he can use it like the spider spinning a web to catch the fly, to keep the reader enmeshed exactly where he wishes. This is linked yet again to rhetoric, the quality of persuasive speech and persuasive writing.

We can all think of magical moments in real life – a child takes his first steps, a visit reconciles you with an old friend, a tree that seemed dried up bursts into flower – just as many of us can recollect miracles. I am not here to preach to you, but the image fits the case. Every flower opening, every chick emerging from the egg, is a magical moment that may be unobserved and so does not work its spell on anyone. So are we conscious of a miracle when passers-by appear in a lonely road where we think we are going to be mugged, when a sick person makes an amazing recovery or a cheque for arrears turns up at a moment when we are desperate because someone else has failed to pay us. We say "Thank God" and feel renewed. But there are other miracles we do not see and recognise. Accidents are averted, bad intentions are thwarted and temptations are overcome. We may not be aware of it. A person of faith lives among miracles, but in giving a testimony, we have to refer to specific cases. Likewise, fictional stories are made up of specific cases in which the ordinary and the extraordinary are mixed. If nothing is extraordinary, there is no story. If nothing is ordinary, we have no way to latch on to the story. We may not interpret correctly. The children in Richard Hughes' novel *High Wind in Jamaica* are more excited by the hurricane, a morally neutral natural event, than by their encounter with the pirates. But, it is this encounter which exposes all kinds of moral implications which the younger children fail to understand. In our own lives, we may not pinpoint, for our children, or ourselves the exact moment which will later come to look decisive, to lead to a certain course of study, a certain marriage, a change of house or job. But in writing the story, the author has to be more sensitive than his characters and to emphasise the irrevocable points of which they may not yet be conscious.

In one way, there are endless stories, more than one for every person born. In another way, there are only a few themes – the hunt, the fight in a narrow place, marriage and procreation, rise and fall. We ring the changes on these endlessly – as bell-ringers do with their few notes. The first time a thing is done perfectly it bowls us over and sets a standard for all attempts that follow.

Chinua Achebe's *Thing's Fall Apart* was something new and staggering of its kind. So was Raja Rao's *Kathnapoori*, the story of the prelude to independence in an Indian village. George Moore's novel *Esther Waters* of 1894 gave a new insight into the condition of women cutting across class and lifestyle. Fresh beginnings like this cannot be expected in every decade or even generation, yet they do often inspire imitators to try new themes or methods, sometimes with success.

Imitation is a good exercise and a tribute to the model. We all seized on Okot P'Bitek's breathless line structure. We all saw Graham Greene's uplifting of the thriller. There is nothing wrong with this so long as there is no actual plagiarism. But, if someone builds on existing work, or quotes many actual lines of poetry, acknowledgement must be made.

Perhaps, it is time to re-examine that word creativity. Everybody who writes at all writes prose, even if it is only an invitation card or a thank you letter. So, there is a continuum of different kinds of prose writing, not all of which are imaginative. Poetry is virtually all creative and even if verse is used in non-poetic ways like advertising, it still has a creative component. But in prose, you have to be aware of the point where you move from the literal to the artistic mode.

Creativity means adding something new to the material out of which you are making your artwork. Once the something new is there, it is part of the whole and can be examined but not removed. The cookery examiner does not take the cake you have baked to the laboratory to determine whether you have used blue band or butter. The cake has to be judged as a cake. When you sit down to write a story, you do not say, "I want to write a first person narrative using reflective paraphrase for the minor characters and reflecting the idiom of Form Two girls in Western Kenya". You say, "I want to write a story about a young man who paid his dowry with stolen cattle and what happened to him and his bride". The technical choices will depend on the nature of the story told, not the other way round. Always remember that without the artist, there would be no work for the critic; without writers there are no publishers.

What has this got to do with themes and images? It shows that even though schools of psychology, theology and political science provide us with ways of looking at events, the artist has to fix his attention on a particular case. John Wain, himself a considerable novelist, quotes Boris Pasternak, the Russian Nobel Prize winner, as saying that art is a statement about life so all embracing that it cannot be split up and that it is the seed of ferment, transfiguring the whole if it is present even in a particle (*Word in the Desert*, 117). I want to stress that statement "*it can't be split up.*" Of course, life can be split up in the sense that we go through different stages as Prof. Eriksson analyses them or our age-sets crystallise them. But our personal memory preserves details which the collective memory or record passes over. Thus, we cannot doubt personal continuity not being split up. And although the statement made by art cannot be split up, a *particle* of it can ferment within a larger whole. That appears to me to mean that while our imperfect attempts may be patchy, the finally achieved work – like the fermented pot of what was originally plain *uji* (porridge) – is assimilated by the art, the fermenting agent. When we look back at the recipe, we may separate the elements – theme, plot, image, background – but when we are actually reading, *absorbed* in the book, we say *soaked* in it, (and this is itself an image), we are at one with it – the separation is not apparent to us.

Song of Lawino burst upon us. Since then, what major ferment have we had? The winner of the Jomo Kenyatta prize does not make the front page of the newspaper or fill the windows of bookshops. AIDS organisations are not urging people to read *The Last Plague* or *Chira*. The search for Dedan Kimathi's grave does not inspire people to re-read Sam Kahiga's novel. Demolitions and security checks go on without drawing on Akare's record in *The Slums*.

John Wain says that *Dr. Zhivago* is a symbolic novel and has the theme of resurrection. That is debatable. All I want to assert here is that when a story is written, subject and theme coalesce – not always perfectly, any more than in human conception, (but most of us believe that human conception is an advance on the amoeba splitting itself into two). Images and symbols attach themselves with various degrees of appropriateness to that coalescence as they do to the upbringing of a human family.

This is in contrast to the Mills and Boon formula which reproduces an identical love story over and over again using different names. Even major writers have to guard against the temptation to repeat and even publishers encourage them to do so.

Let us assume you have now discovered your theme – say the variation in university entrance standards between 1970 and 2000 and you have found the story to fit it: perhaps the son of a 1973 graduate being derided by his father for the things he does not know, not having been through sixth form, when he finishes form IV in 1998. No one has taught him to compile a report from notes as the General Paper used to do. He uses a calculator for what used to be mental arithmetic in standard five. He has not read Ngugi's novels or Angira's poetry. He does not understand all the words used by his grandfather in the ancestral language. He has never looked after cows. On the other hand, he complains that his father has not taken him to the home village often enough to become familiar with life there. His father does not own a computer and has a rather vague idea of how the secretary uses a word processor. He has stayed in the same teaching job for many years. On this thread, it is possible to weave in a varied cast of characters to observe the way different generations and area groups speak, and to say a lot about changes in the country from this narrow base. Think of other examples for yourself.

As well as the actual subject and the theme, there is the sequence of images. This is not easy to talk about. Just as not all poems contain similes and metaphors, not all novels have very obvious images. Therefore, you may not start with a conscious image, but as you constantly rework and recopy your story, you are likely to become aware of the symbols and emblems that can be reapplied in various situations.

I tried to sort out the elements by looking at my own novel *Chira*. AIDS is one of the two *themes* of the book. It is also part of the *subject*, providing the story of victims and how people interact with them. It is also used as an *image* or metaphor of the rot in the political and economic system. These three ways of using the syndrome are all intertwined.

If you look at Dorothy Sayers' excellent suspense and character novel, *The Nine Tailors*, the title refers to a peal of bells housed in an ancient village church. In Kenya, we only hear such peals on record, but in Ethiopia, bells are highly significant. The bells are central to the story because it is the team of ringers and their families, who are among the main characters and, unknown to themselves, precipitate the action. The tolling of one bell also announces a death in the community and occurs several times in the story. They are both subject and image: the theme may be mortality in a place, which through crime has lost its peace.

Writing in 1934, Sayers, herself a clergyman's daughter, could not have known that during the Second World War, the church bells would cease to ring in England, as they were only to be used as a signal of enemy invasion. She may have sensed, all the same, that the village way of life, centering on the church and the gentleman's house, was coming to an end. In this way, *The Nine Tailors* parallels many African novels of social change.

Images may easily be over-worked: think of the dolls' house in V.S. Naipaul's generally fine novel *A house for Mr. Biswas*. In Meja Mwangi's stories of Nairobi, there are frequent descriptions of cockroaches and human waste to indicate the conditions under which people are living. This works when we read them at a distance but in Mathare and Korogocho slum areas, they can be taken for granted. Mwangi's novel *Shaka Zulu*, set in America, is almost like a catalogue of Greyhound Bus Stations, as though to emphasise the impermanence of the scene where people are constantly moving from place to place. Fog, mist, cigarette smoke often appears to signify mystery, deception, and lack of clear vision. Charles Dickens' novels of London keep referring to the fog which characterised any big smoky city before the days of pollution control. The last really bad one in London occurred the day I did my oral interview for MA and from the tower of the Senate House; you could not see the ground below. Dickens also uses the swampy and smelly parts of the city, the docksides and garbage heaps, to give an atmosphere. In *Great Expectations*, with a theme of deception and self-deception, the wasteland and marshes of the Thames estuary where Pip first meets the convict reappears at the end where he desperately tries to save his old friend. It also symbolises the dreary waste of Miss Havisham's life.

I have to be honest and say that when I tried to make a mental review of novels in the African Writers Series only a few came to mind in terms of images as distinct from incidents and characters. For instance, in West Africa, fabrics, related as they are to wealth and social class, are often mentioned. The seasonal migration and the round of the agricultural and industrial year everywhere mark the passage of time.

We have already looked at the management of absent characters in *Wuthering Heights*. The subject is the love between Cathy and Heathcliff. The theme may be irrational behaviour in small closed communities. The recurrent images are of snow and storm and rough landscape putting up barriers between neighbours. The behaviour of the dogs, mirroring the tempers of their masters, is also a significant image.

Landscape and indoor settings are very much part of imagery. In Patrick White's *The Tree of Man,* images of the food the women are cooking indoors or outdoors are used to picture the growing sophistication of settlement in Australia. In R.C. Hutchinson's *Recollections of a Journey*, a story of displacement and suffering during the Second World War, the women mark the stages of loss in terms of clothes and jewels they remember from more comfortable days as more and more of their personal luggage has to be left behind. An image works if it is naturally connected to the story. If it has to be dragged in to make a conscious pattern, it may put the reader off.

When I was typing out this chapter, I got up from my desk to close the curtains and caught sight of dozens of birds wheeling over the market, against the grey sky, preparing to nest for the night. I could not identify the birds, but they all resembled one another, slim, black, and circling repetitively. What an image that would be, I thought, for the close of life, for failing sight, the compulsive patterns being repeated as the light fades. It has been overworked, of course, but still has immediacy for old people.

This image of the birds is almost universal. You can find it in any part of the world, in town and countryside. But many others, even the seaside or riverside, are hard to universalise. When Dickens pictures for us rooms and streets inhabited by his characters, we could find places in Nairobi or Mombasa that would suit the same people if they were reborn in East Africa. But, it is not obvious to me that the characters of Achebe or Sembene Ousmane or Charles Mungoshi or Ayi Kwei Armah could be realised in a Kenyan setting. So, we might have to be careful not to assume the thematic incidents intimate to the landscapes of these novels – the wrestling matches, the libations, the trade union meetings, the special foods – necessarily as symbols. They are a literal part of a way of life just as the bells are in *The Nine Tailors*. In Kenya, these bell ringers would be choir members or students of Theological Education by Extension. The West African masquerades could be guitar-players or football club supporters. In a Ujamaa village, they would be leaders of a hundred houses. There is a potential for symbolism but not all representation is symbolic. You may decide to kill a goat instead of baking a wedding-cake, but in either case, the item is supposed to be good to eat.

Religious ceremonies, of literal significance to many of us, need to be handled carefully even if seen by unbelievers as symptoms of social power structure. They are not only decorative but are also symbolic. The novel is not a currant cake from which you pick out elements of sweetness. It is a richly blended mixture which it takes an educated palate to appreciate as a whole. When a novel is made into a film, visual images gain in importance and precision, and sometimes, the author himself alters the balance to suit the medium. Graham Greene did this several times. The storyteller has to correct his readers' ideas of what is important. We may disagree about what is right or wrong to do, but we usually agree about where a decision is required. When I look back to my childhood reading of the Christian classic *Pilgrim's Progress,* I remember it as dominated by the terrible burden Christian carried which fell off his back, in the basic evangelical image, at the foot of the cross. On revisiting the novel, we find that the burden is lifted quite early in the story and a series of other scriptural pictures, reinforced by folklore elements of giants and cruel landowners carry the narrative on to the gate of the celestial city. That is to say, the dominant image may not be the one that occurs most often, but the one that sets the reader's mind on the track prepared for it. In *The River Between,* the valley between two ridges stands for the meeting-point of two ways of life, rather more literally than people of the place and time actually saw it. But in Margaret Ogola's *The River and the Source,* the reference to the river is proverbial, although it also carries the idea of flow and continuity. So, let us say that the image may have less than symbolic value and yet hold a story together by reminding the reader of an earlier episode.

There is no way to make easy the distinction between theme, subject and image. In poetry, compression of form and common use of metaphor makes it easier to analyse the relation between parts. It is not usual for a whole long fictional work to be read as a metaphor, other than the allegories we have looked at. There are too many variables. Perhaps the novels of Kafka are closest to this and tend to have an airless feeling about them. We know we are not seeing the whole picture. This is typical of writing in societies that are subject to heavy censorship, and so need to offer an alternative explanation of what is being said. Perhaps it is significant that J.M. Coetzee from South Africa, who has twice won the Booker Prize and now the Nobel Prize for his exceedingly depressing stories, learned to write in that vein before the breakdown of apartheid in that country.

Chapter 5

Narrative

A novel tells a story. It may also tell the reader other things such as the author's opinions (as in *The Last Plague*), the circumstances of writing (as in *The Jail Bugs*), a view of history (as in *One Hundred Years of Solitude*) – but if the story does not predominate, it cannot be defined as a novel.

Apart from the related genres discussed in chapter two, there are other kinds of narratives. A doctor's examination of a patient begins with a "history" of her conditions and circumstances. A judge's summing-up of a case starts with the ascertainable facts. A set of accounts may be accompanied by a narration of what has happened in and around the company concerned – a take-over, a rise in exchange rates or tax, a shortage of raw materials, a fire.

I do not remember being told much about narrative methods when I was a student. This is not because our twenty first century "narratology" is inventing any new methods of telling a story that have not been there from time immemorial. Perhaps what is new is a scepticism, an awareness of devious intent, which characterises the second half of the twentieth century. Neither the doubt nor the intent is new. "The hands are the hands of Essau but the voice is the voice of Jacob" (*Genesis* 27:22). We have added emphasis and tedious explanation. When King Solomon advises cutting a disputed baby in halves (1 *Kings* 3: 25), everyone knows that the genuine mother will protest. When the dying King Arthur sends Sir Bedivere back and back again to the edge of the lake, we know that the mystical climax of the story is near. The narrator may have remembered the prophet Elijah sending his servant out repeatedly until he saw the little cloud that forecast the coming rain. Luo rainmakers are also reputed to have told those praying, "Don't stand about gossiping, or the storm will overtake you on the way." The story is not meant to be open-ended. Anglo-Saxon bards kept their listeners to the main theme by repeating the tag, "It was not for the last time." Perhaps it is only the open-ended story that is new, and possibly our ancestors would have seen an open-ended story as simply unfinished.

A story can be told:

- objectively, without intrusion by a narrator. This is sometimes called "the eye of God method." The storyteller knows everything that happens, whether or not the characters know it. Even so, he may decide not to disclose events to the reader in the order in which they occur, as in Patrick White's *Voss*.

- subjectively, still from the eye of God, but implying a judgement on the situation as in Steinbeck's *Grapes of Wrath*.

- by first person narrative, a character in the story telling it as he knows it, sometimes having to fill in background on something after it comes to his knowledge. The narrator may be:
  - a principal actor in the story as in George Lamming's *In the Castle of my Skin*
  - a minor character who participates in but is not a driving force in the story, like the tenant in Emily Bronte's *Wuthering Heights*
  - several characters sharing the narrative, as in Wilkie Collins' *The Woman in White*

- an alternation of the detached narrator and one or more of the characters as in Dickens' *Bleak House*
- a collection of supposed documents, letters, or records.

There are also various kinds of frames used to suggest a reason for telling stories from the 1001 stories of the *Arabian Nights* up to the present, or the series stories like the spider and hare themes in African and African-American folklore or the Renard the Fox theme in northern Europe. Some frames, like those used in the fourteenth century by Chaucer and Boccaccio (without a strong separation of verse and prose narrative) add to the fun. Some, like Hawthorne's elaborate run-up to *The Scarlet Letter*, jar on the modern ear.

I do not believe that most writers begin by making a deliberate choice of narrative method, though a choice will have to be made somewhere along the way while the material is still fluid. Sometimes, an experienced storyteller, like an experienced poet, may set out to try his hand at a new mode. So, we may have several tries before finding the exact narrative voice we want. I had planned to write *Murder in Majengo* in very simple sentences, but I was not able to do so. In *The Present Moment,* I changed several times the order of disclosure of what the reader needed to know, although for most of the book, the reader knows things that some of the old ladies in the Refuge do not.

In several of his books, William Golding, whose *Lord of the Flies* was once a set book for O-level, keeps an important disclosure till the very last page. I do not think this is a good strategy. In real life if we find out, perhaps only when someone dies, what his real position in the family is, we are uncomfortable and would like to pose questions which now cannot be answered. In Golding's *The Spire,* we are told at last that the bishop is the son of the king. This must have been known to many of the monks and builders in the story. It explains his early promotion and command of funds. Why should the reader be kept in ignorance? A more reasonable scenario occurs when some characters are kept in ignorance of what some others do know but have a reason for not telling. For instance, in Dickens' *Tale of Two Cities,* readers know that Sidney Carton is not the man in whose name he is being executed. But the substitution would not work if the executioners knew of it or even if the threatened family knew it, because they would not accept the sacrifice of his life. In Wahome Mutahi's *Three Days on the Cross,* we are presented with Momodu and Chipota in their imprisonment, but their wives and employers do not know where they are. It is only later that a situation allowing possible escape can be set up.

Sometimes, the topic of the story is there only by implication behind the events described. In Zoe Wicomb's *Another Story*, the young, "so-called coloured" historian asks questions which seem valueless to her great-aunt Deborah, a spinster housekeeper. Sarah is arrested, but what has happened to Deborah, with her fine cooking and her weekly white woman's "book," implies the history that we are so sketchily told (Lefanu and Heyward).

Another decision has to be made about the amount of detail required in a narrative. As a rule, description should be kept to a minimum necessary to enable the reader to picture the surroundings, but when different cultures meet, a lot is disclosed by naming the items that surprise the newcomer. With an international audience, there is a temptation to over-explain, but most of us can deduce the function of articles (sufuria, epergne, wok, billy) from the context and of titles (foreman, naval rating, aide-de-camp, Bayete) from the way they are used. Concepts of space and size are often subjective and comparisons can tell us a lot about the character. Trees may seem to one person soaring like cathedrals, to another enclosing a tunnel of darkness. The notion of "river" or "stream" holds different content in different languages. A point of view is implicit in what can be taken for granted, what needs explanation. Prices in remote times and places need to be related discreetly to possible earnings. So, historians tell us that Jesus' disciples were estimating a working man's wages for eight months as the cost of a small snack for 5000 people. In Toni

Morrison's *Beloved,* the girl from Denver is crossing America with the aim of getting a piece of velvet fabric of a particular colour. Her imagination is not more demanding than that.

Within any of the forms of narrative outlined above, the narrator may use devices which either expand the scope or mark time, indicating the passing of events or absence of them until something significant to the main action resurfaces. For instance, in *Coming to Birth,* Paulina has to establish a routine in which she keeps busy and learns to live with her grief in the years between Okeyo's death and her reunion with Martin. Such devices may be:

- *The flashback.* This is used frequently by Genga Idowu in her novels. Care has to be taken that the reader does not get the time schemes confused. John Le Carre uses the flashback masterfully.

- *The interior monologue*: this is chiefly useful when the circumstances of the story do not allow means to demonstrate the thought in action. For instance, I use it in *Homing In* to explore the memories of a woman who has had a stroke. The hallucinations of "The Fixer" on his way to execution in Bernard Malamud's novel tell us more about imperial Russian society than a straight narrative could. This is called the "stream of consciousness" method. Where it is used as the main vehicle, as in William Faulkner's *The Sound and the Fury*, the major story-line is left for the reader to deduce from scattered fragments of memory and the time-sequence is hard to interpret. Most writers vary the method to give the audience a bit more help.

- *The story within a story*: like the "Hymn to the Sun" in Chinua Achebe's *Anthills of the Savannah.*

- Interruption of the time sequence, as in A.S. Byatt's *Possession.*

- Mistaken identification of characters by the protagonists as in Ishiguro's *When we Were Orphans.*

- *Intertextuality*, that is, cross-reference, from one work to another the reader is expected to recognise. This has continued from ancient times when Virgil picked an incident from the Greek poems of Homer to open his *Aeneid* to modern times when Jean Rhys in *The Wide Sargasso Sea* imagines the action preceding Charlotte Bronte's *Jane Eyre* and Peter Carey uses whole pages of out of copyright work to pad out his novels.

None of these devices is new. *Tristram Shandy* by Laurence Sterne (issued in parts 1770-1777), with its innuendo, its typographical jokes, its constant procrastination of the supposed story of the nephew's birth, its ebullient character-drawing, has many of the features sometimes called "post-modern." It has been said that Sterne "invented for English literature the fantasia-novel" and "left the novel the most flexible of literary forms," (*The Shorter Cambridge History of English Literature*, pp.510). The terrible ironies and physicality of Swift also strike a chord with the 20th century – Lilliput and Brobdignag are only a preface to the true horrors of *Gulliver's Travels* (1726).

All these methods indicate stages in the release of information. This, as we have already seen from Paul Scott's handling of themes, is the key to the relationship between the writer's mind and the reader's.

Let us look at the detective story, for example. This is a kind of narrative that can operate at any level of complexity, and has been favoured by several literary dons and clergymen writing under pseudonyms. The story aims at solving the mystery of a crime or act of espionage, even if the reader is able to identify the person responsible from the beginning. For instance, John Banville's creation of the life of the spy related to the royal family, Sir Anthony Blunt, *The Untouchable*, is a masterly evocation of place and period. The official version of Blunt's career is already known.

Since in a detective story the reader's enjoyment comes largely from pitting his wits against the investigators', a great deal of irrelevant information has to be inserted (as also happens in real life) so that incorrect leads will be followed up before the truth emerges. The artistry lies in keeping this interesting because it throws light on the characters involved. In *The Constant Gardener*, Le Carre's novel of Kenya, there is no sexual relationship between Tessa and Arnold, but the fact that people think there is affects the action. Some detective writers like P.D. James tend to introduce excessive detail related to their personal tastes. Some, like Raymond Chandler, one of the most sensitive writers to use this form, select such details – intrusive make-up that girls use to distance themselves from reality, the shabby offices in which confidential deals are brokered – to sketch a whole marginal society and show how it is conducive to evil-doing. Some insult our intelligence by dragging in weapons or motives that the previous story has given no clue to. My own *Murder in Majengo* is not in that sense a detective story. Crimes in our urban slums do not ordinarily have neat solutions any more than murders in the similarly intricate thickets of high politics. Making an arrest does not necessarily explain anything.

So, in the subtler regions of the social novel, to expose a situation does not prevent its recurring. The sequence of events may seem inevitable as in Sam Kahiga's *Dedan Kimathi: The Real Story*, while in the same writer's *Paradise Farm,* the events revealed at the end seem not to be implicit in the whole story.

A character's behaviour may be influenced by what she knows or comes to know about other people. For instance, at the beginning of *Bleak House*, Esther Summerson does not know that she is the daughter of Lady Dedlock. Nor does the reader know it, though he does know that the two families have an interest in the same case in the court of Chancery. The actions of the characters are more interesting than past revelations. Small mysteries like the identity of Trooper George can easily be guessed. In Meja Mwangi's *The Last Plague*, the HIV status of Frank Fundi remains a puzzle until near end of the book.

In many cases, the order of disclosure of information is crucial and the author may have several changes of mind before getting it right. So, let us look at the example given earlier in the *Themes* chapter about a Kenyan novel of father and son and their approach to university.

- You may start it with a third person narrator recording a dialogue between father and son and then going to the story of the son's life with his father, putting in stories of the past from time to time.

- You may start with such a dialogue and follow with a flashback to the father's relations with his own parents as he aspired to higher education, and an interior monologue of the son thinking about his own parents.

- You may tell the story in the son's voice, cutting back to what his father says or what he supposes his father to think. In this case, you reduce the possibility of a realistic portrayal of his father's and grandfather's generation.

- You may have the father tell the story, in which case the son's point of view will be mediated, except insofar as dialogue from his own generation may be literally reported (even if misunderstood by the father). Such dialogue will seem dated if your novel is still being read twenty years later.

- You may have another narrator, for instance, a younger sister of the father, who regrets not having had the same chances and yet has a sufficiently fulfilled life to report all sides of the action. She will probably see more likeness between father and son than either of them sees of themselves.

- You may wish to make ironical comment by inserting actual documents of different dates on education policy or resources.

Of course, there are many other possibilities. In choosing among them, you will be motivated partly by what is possible in terms of the information you have or have access to. You may desire to put on record a particular point of view of someone you admire or to refrain from causing pain to that person. You may wish to advocate a particular policy or to celebrate the different pleasures of learning. You may have a particular register of speech in mind.

You will need time and experiment to come to a decision. That decision will determine the title of the novel. Not all choices are academic. I planned to write *A Farm called Kishinev* in three parts, to be narrated by grandfather, son and grandson. I had to restrict my ambitions because I was no longer physically able to complete all the research I had intended. So, I decided that the grandson's voice would enable me to comment on events up to date, while still drawing on memories or documents of an earlier generation. I was also influenced by the fact that some questions put to different informants elicited incompatible answers, and even historical descriptions did not agree. This means not that one guess is as good as another but that a certain amount of intuitive guessing is inevitable. It helps to remind us that not all generalisations are meaningful. There never was "an English wedding" or "a Luo funeral." There is always a component special to the circumstances. But this does not mean that no historical facts are verifiable, as extreme post-modernists may assert. If you have evidence that a certain item was advertised at a certain price in a named township at a given date, that a person of known community and religious affiliation was engaged as a teacher at that time and place, that the Official Gazette was at the same time circulating information about a will, a bankruptcy, a wage schedule or an outbreak of foot and mouth disease, then you have a framework for a picture of that society.

The events of your story may not have commonly happened but they could have happened and the framework supplements what the memories of old people may have slightly distorted. Your character could have got a job, she could have owned a tilley-lamp, she could have known that her previous employer had recently disembarked at Mombasa, she could have been baptised by an

African clergyman, she could have travelled by train to a specific station, and she could have sent a money order.

The first page of any piece of work has a great deal to do with whether the reader goes on paying attention or not. The last page has a lot to do with whether he has further questions to ask (which may be the writer's intention), whether the reading has accomplished the drawing together of personalities and emotions, cause and effect, that is, the meat of the story; also whether there is a resolution, a right relationship between parts, what it is fashionable these days to call closure, the completion of an experience.

It is because stories engage our sympathy as well as our intellect that this is a technical exercise of considerable delicacy. We may get satisfaction at the end of a theorem in geometry – QED. There is satisfaction in opening a textbook and finding on the first page a statement of intention, such as "I propose to examine the assumptions governing international loans to corporate bodies." Now we know where we are. There is satisfaction when an author starts by relating his subject to other spheres of knowledge. "The universal is the local without walls," as Professor Harper puts it.

But in a novel or a short story where a scene is being set out of an infinite number of possible scenes, and characters brought alive out of a terrifying range of possible characters, there is no standard way of focusing the reader's attention. Each time we do it, we reduce the number of unused possibilities. Sometimes we have to draw on or repeat other people's openings. This is where the writer stands on the still bare stage fixing the audience's attention like Brother Jero in Wole Soyinka's play, "There are eggs and eggs. Same thing with prophets." We have already looked at the narrative method of *Wuthering Heights*. In the opening scene, the new tenant of Thrush cross Grange calls on his landlord at Wuthering Heights. This gives him reason to cross the grim countryside, look at the forbidding exterior of the house and introduce himself. That way, we learn why he has come to stay in so lonely an area and see through his eyes the strange characters that live at the Heights. This is an excellent technique for setting the scene and whetting the reader's appetite.

The *short story* is a much more difficult form than the novel because the narrative must be able to achieve its goal in a few pages. The setting must be demonstrated, leaving out everything extraneous to the story, and the point made in a paragraph or two. I do not write short stories myself, since the few I tried when I was young made me feel that each required as much imaginative labour as a whole novel. A novella is "an in between length", usually between 40 and 70 pages, in which a story with small cast of characters can be worked out. It is, therefore, seldom able to analyse a situation as deeply as a full novel. My own work, *Street Life,* is a novella published in aid of charity. I had wanted to write full novel in dialogue form, looking at things from pavement level, but found that was too hard, so I used up some of the dialogues in the novella. Some people issue linked short stories as an in-between form. Sir Arthur Conan Doyle's many stories about the detective Sherlock Holmes and his friend Dr. Watson are among the most famous and are still good readings despite their old-fashioned setting. If we had as good a telegraph services as London had in 1890s, we might not have to use our mobile phones!

This is the first paragraph of Grace Ogot's story "The Empty Basket" from her collection *Land Without Thunder,* 1998:

> Aloo hastened her steps. She felt nervous and panicky. It looked as though the earth under her feet was moving in the way that angry clouds race in the sky when it is going to rain. But now the earth was moving in the opposite direction pushing the hut further and further away. She started running. The distance was narrowing. She could see more people gathered in the yard close to the hut. She recognised Nariwo, the wife of her brother-in-law whose hut was in the village next to theirs. Aloo's knees suddenly went weak and numb, and she could not run. (pp.79).

We soon find that a big snake has entered the bedroom of Aloo's house where her baby girl is asleep. The skilful evocation of Aloo's growing fear and the transfer of that menace to the surroundings and the weather– what is technically called the pathetic fallacy – winds up the reader's feelings and leads to the solution of the problem in a concise and memorable manner. In a novel, the suspense would have to be sustained over a long period.

Another issue to consider is *the stage you begin to write*. Paul Scott has shown us that the conception is in your mind before anything goes down on the page. The words come later and may be reshuffled and re-written many times, as the plot develops.

We meet people as we relate to them and little by little find out what they did before and who their relations are. Often, we never find it out. The first chapter of a novel sets us in a relationship to the characters and the story gradually reveals more about them. The same with events. We know that a bomb went off in Nairobi in 1998, that there was fighting in Iraq in 2003, that Kenya got independence in 1963, but to get interested in the narrative, we have to see how these events relate, from page one, to the protagonists. If the events are fictional – a fire, a murder, a coup – or literally, true, but so far removed from the expected reader's consciousness that they have to be explained, then they have to be introduced as part of the story, not a history lesson or a foot-note.

This is where the writer's sense of design comes into play, shaping the idea that is already in his mind. Just as a poem is recognisable by its pattern of sounds, so a story is distinguished from a jumble of news items by keeping the parts in relation to one another and fixing them in the reader's memory. This is like music, where different styles and images interweave at different speeds.

In most cases, as Paul Scott has said, the end is pre-determined. It is part of the idea of the book. In my own case, I usually, not always, start with the beginning and the end: how does a person who, you know started in this circumstance end up in that one?

Someone else may start with a public situation – a battle or an accident – and go on to trace how it affects people's separate lives and brings them together. Or it is possible to start with a person looking back over the years and recounting some incidents, as Stefanie does in R.C Hutchinson's *Recollection of a Journey*, not always in the order they happened but in the order she came to know about them.

These are the given points: imagination and research work upon the process of change. So, the end depicts a staging post in the characters' lives, and usually, this corresponds with a point in the theme which the characters illustrate – perhaps a war has ended or begun, the economic system has been revised, a new technology is taking over or there is a revival in the church. When I planned *Coming to Birth*, relating Paulina's personal experience to the tremendous excitement of the early independence period, I intended it to cover 20 years, 1956 to 1976. Before I had finished writing it, President Kenyatta had died, and it was obvious that 1978, with a change in government, was the appropriate cut-off point. It did not make a fundamental difference: Paulina was 38 instead of 36, still able to carry through her pregnancy successfully. It just entailed filling in a little more background. The cut-off point may be either a real life event or a fictional one.

The commonest fictional endings relate to the solution of a mystery or a situation – a conflict, a courtship or a change of mind. When the end is inconclusive, it may be that another piece of work to extend the action and the development of the characters is forming in the writer's mind. Other novelists, like Bernard Malamud or Thomas Keneally, embody the theme they want to resolve in new stories relating to quite different times and places. It would be a useful study to compare the end positions of such sets of novels.

A recent critic has said of D.H. Lawrence, the mid 20th century novelist who insisted to the point of boredom in bringing explicit sex into the English novel: "that rhythmic, seductive, irritatingly repetitive style... leads us to what can best be described as a catharsis of exhaustion" [2]

Tim Parks gives the example of *Women in Love*, ending with a wrestling match that neither contestant wins. These are the final sentences of *Sons and Lovers*, Lawrence's close to autobiographical novel. The protagonist's mother has died and he has rejected the possibility of marriage:

> Night, in which everything was lost, went reaching out, beyond stars and sun. Stars and sun, a few bright grains, went spinning round for terror, and holding each other in embrace, there in a darkness that outpassed them all, and left them tiny and daunted. So much, and himself infinitesimal, at the core of nothingness, and yet not nothing.
> 'Mother!' he whispered – 'mother!'
> She was the only thing that held him up, himself, amid all this. And she was gone, intermingled herself. He wanted her to touch him, have him alongside with her.
> But no, he would not give in. Turning sharply, he walked towards the city's gold phosphorescence. His fists were shut, his mouth set fast. He would not take that direction, to the darkness, to follow her. He walked towards the faintly humming, glowing town, quickly. (*Sons and Lovers*, Penguin 1948, 510f)

Nothing is solved, but a mood is created. In Lawrence's books, sex is almost divorced from having children and building a community. People are loners.

Jane Austen says near the end of *Northanger Abbey*, "my readers... will see in the tell-tale compression of the pages before them, that we are all hastening together to perfect felicity", p.234. This is ironic, of course. Jane Austen was unmarried herself and

---

[2] (Catharsis – purging, cleaning out, in the sense that Aristotle described out emotions as being emptied by watching a dramatic tragedy. (Tim Parks in *New York Review of Books* (NYRB) 25.9.03).

was a member of a large family. She knew very well, as her stories show us, that few marriages are totally happy and many, in those days of slow transport and limited technology, extremely boring. But modest expectations reap modest rewards. The story ends with the expectation that those concerned will be as happy as society considers normal.

In a realistic type of novel, which was the mainstream for the 18th, 19th and much of the 20th century, we are disappointed if the end is not in keeping with the whole sweep of the narrative. Thackeray, the 19th century author of *Vanity Fair*, works through the battle of Waterloo and the whole social and economic scene of the period he is recreating to bring about the marriage of Dobbin and Amelia. It was happy, he says, it was notably good for the son of Amelia's first marriage, but it was not quite as rapturous as Dobbin, after his long years of courtship, had expected. This is not surprising, given our knowledge of the characters. We feel the author is being honest with us.

In some other cases, the allegedly happy ending leaves us a bit uncomfortable. Then there is a whole genre of adventure novels where the hero struggles to complete his mission, only to find that he has been deceived about the real purpose. It needs delicate handling to keep the reader aware of possible reversal of intentions all the way through. The twist in the tail ought not to be quite unanticipated.

We can never tell it all. That is the nature of the real world. Our aim has been to bring the story to a close that will satisfy the reader's curiosity, keep up his concern and cause him to reflect on the events and feelings he has shared. Then we withdraw.

Chapter 6

Getting Published

Here I want to look at some of the stages that lie between the private desk copy and the printed book, with a glance at other forms of publishing. We are all impatient for our first efforts to see the light of day. So are thousands of eager beavers in every country in the world. It is, therefore, necessary to have an idea of how the publishing industry works. All of us have subsidiary means of communicating what we have to say through private copies, local magazines or performances. A big distributor will demand strictly defined, even if not exclusive, rights and we must be prepared to take advice on the legal interpretation of these and to clamp down on any unauthorised copying.

When you submit copy to a publisher, be prepared for delay. This is a fact of life anywhere in the world. You will get a receipt that tells you to expect a reply in something like three months, but you can start sending reminders after six months and it is very unusual to get an acceptance within a year. In America, it is common to make a number of copies of your manuscript and send it to several publishers at once. In Britain, where I grew up, this would be considered very rude (though agents have their own methods of work) and I still feel it is so. You expect that the publisher, after first weeding out whatever is either hopeless or inappropriate to his list, will spend time and money getting several people to report on the remaining manuscripts, after careful reading. There will then be an editorial conference to consider their recommendations, a calculation of the cost of producing what is selected and possibly, a rejection of someone else's writing on the same topic in favour of your own. It is hardly fair to withdraw the submission at this stage. It is like a breach of promise. But you can refuse the offer if it is inadequate or demands more changes than you are prepared to make in the work.

Nobody told me when I was young to enclose the pages in a file, and we had no facilities yet for ring binding, photocopy or fancy print. Everything had to be typed with a carbon, and that technology is not much more than 100 years old. Before that, companies would employ a school-leaver to copy out typed letters into a letter-book by hand! What is important is to keep the manuscript pages in the right order.

You must always keep a copy, preferably an exact duplicate. At one time, I sent off an urgently requested manuscript without pasting up the copy to the same pagination, and was greatly embarrassed when an inexperienced editor cut up the top copy with scissors and could not get it back into the right order. Nowadays, photocopies are a great blessing and can mask joins and whiteouts in the worked-over manuscript. Clear return instructions and postage must accompany every submission. You can buy UNESCO reply coupons from GPO for copies that may have to be returned from overseas. Young people will know better than I do the risks involved in posting a diskette or a CD.

On his side, the publisher should safeguard your manuscript, protect it from anyone who might misuse or copy, it and not make any mark on it until he has accepted it and offered a contract. This is important because it is not unknown for backroom deals to be made even by the staff of publishing houses, and for amateur readers to offer incredibly inept "corrections". The publisher is not bound to give any reasons for refusal, but he may do so, and this can be helpful to the author. Remember that the publisher is in business and it is not a business in which large fortunes are made. If he has just accepted one manuscript about, say, the Mungiki Movement, he cannot go into competition with himself by accepting another, even if it is a better one. His publishing budget allows so many books covering different topics within the financial year and that is it. He also may have a standard length for a particular series of books, or a graded vocabulary, and may advise writers about this.

The author should not pay an editor to go through the work because this comes at a later stage and has to conform to the house style of the particular publisher in, for instance, spacing, headings and indentation of paragraphs. Normally, the author should not be asked to pay the publisher for editorial work, and is entitled to reject any which he believes incompatible with the style or message of the work, though this may lead to rejection by the publisher. The author may be required to pay for artwork incorporated in the book though not for the cover design. Any such fee will be deducted from payments made on the book.

Steep rises in paper prices and freight costs have entirely changed the formula for estimating the viable cost of a book over the last 25 years in all countries and we have to be realistic about this.

A textbook may be written with an eye to a particular publisher's series, or a juvenile to a specific series format. If this is so, it is wise to put up a proposal before you have sacrificed very much time for it. Some also may be commissioned, but be warned: unless there is a precise contract, a verbal suggestion that you might follow up a previous story or explore a field of interest, does not bind the publisher to anything. Most books, however, grow through interest and opportunity rather than from a precise intention to place them in a list. So when your book is ready, to make its way, you need to know the fields of interest of different publishers, what topics they are best known for, what readership they aim at, how good their distribution system is, how seriously they are taken by the intellectual community. The same applies to periodicals. In Kenya, we do not have much choice but we must keep on pressing for at least pan-African exchange of journals so that we get a wider market and also do not duplicate what is being done elsewhere. The standing of a publisher or magazine can be pretty well judged by which papers review their productions.

You can find out these points by reading a selection of books from a publisher and what people say about them. If you are in the trade, you can practically guess the publisher of a book by the look and feel of it. What you will *NOT* find out this way is how they treat their authors – for instance, whether they hold a manuscript pending until they have prepared a different one on the same topic and then return it when the market is already spoiled (yes, unfortunately this can happen) whether they pay somewhere near the date agreed in the contract, whether they interpret a contract fairly and whether you can trust the sales figures they give you. These things you can only find out by talking with other authors. Moreover, a publishing house is a legal entity and the policy of one executive may be changed by his successor.

Generally, Kenyan publishers are a small and friendly group who know one another and their authors but we look for expansion in this as in other industries. And the international trade is less small, less friendly and has long experience in exploiting ambiguities. Most Kenyan publishers mean well, but newcomers need to be wary of the small print.

The work of professional writers' associations should include helping new writers understand their contracts and claim their rights. We are often, unfortunately, so taken up with grandiose statements that the basic needs are ignored. There is also need of advice on copyright law, particularly in the area of translation rights. Copyright deals with the correct apportionment of earnings, but one of its functions is to protect the writer from being *mis-*

translated or *mis*-copied. We can be liable for prosecution for something we did not write, and I have known even reputable journals omit a *not*, thereby reversing the meaning of a sentence. There is an association attempting to impose a fee on photocopying of copyright works, but this, as our fellow-artists in music can demonstrate, is almost impossible to implement.

The contract should also specify rights in respect of reprints, radio, film and so on. But to be honest, with the technical facilities now available, it is almost impossible to prevent pirating. I remember a Kenyan publisher telling me that an Indian publisher had pressed him for rights in a textbook at a very low price, which would leave hardly anything for the Kenyan author, and publisher. When he protested, he was told, "If you refuse, I shall do the reprint anyway and I shall have sold it out and made my profit before you can bring a case against me."

The best safeguard against this sort of thing is for our own publishers to promote our books in neighbouring countries or sublet them in joint publication schemes. Further a field, it is difficult to be sure traders are not claiming rights they do not have.

The ideal situation in a small but experienced publishing economy like Kenya's is for a local publisher to lease reprint rights for overseas books in demand as we do for some of the African Writers' Series and print and sell the books on the spot. This creates jobs in printing and distribution and saves on freight costs. Only a fair fee for the foreign publisher has to be paid in foreign currency and royalty returns will be made through that publisher.

A publisher will generally give you 10% of the trade price of the book. It used to be 10% of the selling price, so if you are very lucky, you may get 12.5% of the trade price. This change has occurred because British law has reduced publishers' control over the selling-price and this practice has been followed in many English-speaking countries. The trade price in Kenya will be something between 20% and 33% less than the cover price. In

America, discounts are higher. I have been a bookseller most of my working life and I can assure you that these discounts are what a bookseller really needs to be able to offer a wide display of titles, some of which will never be sold. An author needs the bookseller to make his work visible to the public.

But authors must be vigilant. It has been known for an overseas publisher to invoice his books at much less than the agreed price claiming that this is a subsidy to Africa. If it is a "subsidy", it is at the expense of the author, who is getting very much less than the agreed price and cannot afford to employ an accountant to check how many sales are being made at contract price overseas.

When the manuscript is accepted, and any agreed alterations made, the publisher must pay an advance and you should insist on this, even if it is only 1000 shillings, as it puts your book into the financial records and the accountant will be asking what has been received against this payment. If a commercial body, as distinct from a charity, says, "We do not give advances," check its procedures very carefully. The public sometimes thinks the author is getting something for nothing, because large sums of money are occasionally paid to people like film stars to persuade them to put their name on the publisher's list. But what professional writers get is an advance on *sales*, not an advance on the *work* that has been done long before. The amount is negotiable; I think it should not be less than the selling price of 100 copies, but in practice I have never got that much from a Kenyan publisher. Some try to offer the same amount, for instance, if a book now sells for 300/= as they used to offer when it sold for 40/=.

The advance on overseas publications may look to us like a godsend, but it may not look very good to an author in that country with a higher cost of living. There is always a time gap between publishing and selling enough copies to cover the advance. This may be as long as three years, but it may not be a bad bargain if the advance buys you enough time to get ahead with your next project.

l. – preliminary pages are numbered in Roman figures, if at all – right-hand pages all have odd numbers and left-hand pages even numbers. This is important if you need to leave a space between sections or put illustrations in it. Do not let anyone kid you that the computer cannot make a mistake – its operator can.

Your contract will define for which part of the market you have given the publisher control over your copyright – Kenya, East Africa, Africa, World. You are able to negotiate separately for the other part, but to begin with, you will need professional help. The transfer of rights means that within the territory assigned, anyone wishing to use a substantial passage from your books (e.g. to reprint a poem in an anthology) should pay a fee to the publisher, who will pass on a specified proportion to the author. But it is difficult to enforce this.

SELF-PUBLISHING is a very expensive business: some people call it *Desktop Publishing* but although you can print something on a desk you can only make it public through the market place. Even if you have the money to print and bind copies, you need a distributor to market the book for a percentage, perhaps, a publishing group or a wholesaler. It is not only that doing your own promotion for a few books costs nearly as much as doing it for a large number, it is also true that the bookseller is reluctant to write one order, one cheque, one stock entry, one ledger entry for a single item instead of 50 items from a big publisher.

So much for book rights. Periodical rights are harder to describe because they are less often defined by contract. If you write regularly for a magazine there may be an understanding about fees and frequency of contributions, but generally, there is no obligation to publish what has not been asked for, and topical items go stale very quickly. If your poem is printed in a magazine, you should get a fee on a first rights basis: that is, the copyright remains your own, and the same is true for an anthology of works by different poets. An article in a newspaper or magazine is generally regarded as exclusive unless permission is given to reprint or syndicate it (like the articles by Jonathan Power we see in the *Nation*). One of the drawbacks of periodical publication is that you rarely get proofs on which to correct any mistakes that may creep in, unless it is a scholarly journal. Such journals do not ordinarily pay a fee but will give off prints of your article, which you can use as references for jobs or other submissions.

Interviews on radio and TV are regarded as advertisements to your advantage so they are not paid for, but you may receive an audio or videotape. It may happen that you get a form from an international radio service asking permission to use a piece on some named programme, and hear no more after giving permission. When you try to follow up, you are told that the programme has not yet been aired, and it is virtually impossible to check outside the country.

However, there is no loss to your sales, as it is likely that someone hearing the programme in one language or another may attempt to buy the book. If, however, you sign a similar release for an anthology, it should be possible to determine whether it is published: you should receive the fee agreed for one-time use and, ideally, a copy so that you can check that it has been transcribed or translated correctly.

On-line publishing is a new and expanding field on which I am not competent to comment. Young writers should be exploring new processes and opportunities.

As well as advertising a book and offering it to bookshops, a publisher has a duty to send review copies to literary magazines and newspapers. A reviewer is supposed to give the correct title, author, publisher, date and price of the book. We often find books identified only by the bookshops that carry them. The reader should know what to expect from different publishers. The reviewer should identify the genre of the book and how satisfactory the author's performance is. That is, a first year textbook of economics will not be reviewed in the same terms as an original work presenting new theories. The reviewer is not supposed to use his slot to write an original article on the subject, though he may wish to do that on another occasion. The review is meant to appraise the item on sale to the public (it should be published when the book is on sale locally). We often read reviews of imported books but not many Kenyan books are reviewed overseas unless they have won a prize or otherwise attracted attention.

An editor should keep a file of all reviews and publicity materials connected with the book and ideally copy it to the author to assist him in evaluating his audience. Since this does not happen in practice, the author would be wise to keep his own. Ideally, any publicity about the author should help sell the book. It is extraordinary to me that booksellers no longer give window displays to the winners of the Jomo Kenyatta or Commonwealth prizes or even appears to know who they are! Authors may visit bookshops to follow up their stocks tactfully, but not to excessively.

I read in (Daniel Mendelssohn *New York Review of Books* 13 May, 2004) that a poem commissioned by Augustus (who was not yet emperor) for the triumphant Roman festival of 17 BC was only identified as the work of the poet Horace when a stone tablet recording the fact was found in 1890 AD and committed to a museum. It must have been part of an inscription informing the public about the programme, the equivalent of an electronic message on a screen today. (The date and nature of the festival are recorded in a later History by Suetonius). I wonder whether our present technology would allow us to make such an identification 1900 years after the event. One wonders whether all those anonymous essays we sent to Millennium competitions are circulating somewhere and earning royalties, having been translated into Kirghiz or Tagalog. Shall we ever know? And how?

But I wonder even more how skilled critics and Latinists through all those centuries could have failed to attribute those elegant, taut Sapphic verses to their actual author. The technical will take us so far, but it has to be infused with literary sensibility.

Chapter 7

Analysis of Prose Passages

The reader should study the passages below and look up references before consulting the writer's notes which follow. These could be a basis for group discussion.

The Passages

1. From **Daniachew Worku**, *The Thirteenth Sun*, Ethiopia. African Writers Series, 1973

The Awakening
Goyton

Already, the heavens had begun to grow coldly grey. It was the early dawn when the completeness of the silence attunes the soul to special sensibility, when the stars seem to be hanging strangely close to earth, and when the air breathes chilly, and men cuddle themselves up and sleep soundest.

From the top of the mountain, pure, clear, distinct as if bathed in the freshness of the moment, came the sounds of the church bell: first, only single sounds, then coming faster and faster until they floated and stayed on the air for a while. And then, after a moment of silence, the last series of trembling notes, one stroke after another, echoing themselves through the purple dawn like some kind of sad booming sigh.

Faint streaks of light began to reach heavenward. Red wisps of cloud drifted above the rim of the lake. A raven flapped across the face of the flushed and glowing sun. The night chill relaxed and a genial warmth penetrated forest, hills and huts. The day had begun.

Each man and woman, before bending to reach the water at the lake, pulled a handful of grass and cast it upon the water, then washed hands and face and headed up to the church.

And our hearts filled with the bitterish fresh scents, the delicious coolness of the morning, the mists enveloping the whole lower landscape and most of the far-off mountains, and the loud and resolute songs of the priests – a mixture of a sob, a laugh, and a cry of dread, which sounded like a moan, desperately trying to break into a melody. So, we entered the churchyard.

The district chief came along after us on his trotting mule. Stirrup leather of bullock skin. Crupper and girth of bullock skin. Bridle and headstall of twisted hide. The red saddle cloth flapping in the wind. Trappings jingling with metal pendant and bells. A young man trotting at the right side of the master's mule. A gun in bright satin case over his shoulder. Another man trotting in front of the master's mule, crying, 'Out of the way! Out of the way!' The master dismounted in the churchyard. A red cover was immediately thrown over the animal, reaching from the ears to the fetlocks. A protective measure against the evil eye. I followed the master with my eyes. And his mule too. He looked at all of us for a moment as if On-line we were specks of dust in the yard. His loose drawers extended to just under the knee, where they fitted tight, and were gathered round his waist by a thong or a belt.

A loose shirt over it, and an embroidered damask on top of that. And over the damask, a fur tippet. And on his head, a hat made of straw and grass. And in his hand a white horse tail with a wood handle.

And why shouldn't I? I went closer to the church wall as he did. And like him, I started to pray. He was district chief with his own fertile land. With streams swiftly flowing through it. With natural pastures of long grass interspersed with flowering shrubs. Herds of horned cattle and droves of horses and mules. His own abyss – maze of peaks, ridges, canyons, cliffs and rock spires. I prayed like he prayed. A district chief. He has his scribe with a raw-hide case containing pen and ink. His cottage. Even his own villa.

2. By **Sol Plaatje**, 1875-1932, a gifted S. African writer, interpreter and linguist of Barolong origin. The passage is from *Native Life in South Africa*, 1916.

Persecution of Coloured Women in the Orange 'Free' State

> *Ripe persecution like the plant*
> *Whose nascence Mocha boasted*
>
> *Some bitter fruits produced, whose worth*
> *Was never known till roasted*

When the 'Free' State ex-Republicans made use of the South African constitution – which Lord Gladstone says is one after the Boer sentiment – to ruin the coloured population, they should at least have confined their persecution to the male portion of the blacks (as is done in a milder manner in the other three Provinces), and have left the women and children alone. According to this class legislation no native woman in the Province of the Orange 'Free' State can reside within a municipality whether with or without her parents, or her husband unless she can produce a permit showing that she is a servant in the employ of a white person, this permit being signed by the town clerk. All repressive measures under the old Republic (which, in matters of this kind, always showed a regard for the suzerainty of Great Britain) were mildly applied. Now, under the union, the Republicans are told by the Imperial authorities that since they are self-governing, they have the utmost freedom of action, including freedom to do wrong, without any fear of Imperial interference. Of this licence, the white inhabitants of the Union are making the fullest use. Like a mastiff long held in the leash, they are urging the application of all the former stringent measures enacted against the blacks, and the authorities, in obedience to their electoral supporters, are enforcing these measures with the utmost rigour against the blacks because they have no votes.

Hence, whereas the pass regulations were formerly never enforced by the Boers against clergymen's wives or against the families of respectable native inhabitants, now a minister's wife has not only to produce pass on demand, but, like every woman of colour, she has to pay a shilling for a fresh pass at the end of the month, so that a family consisting of, say, a mother and five daughters pay the municipality 6s every month, whether as a penalty for the colour of their skins or a penalty for their sex it is not clear which.

There is some unexplained anomaly in this woman's pass business. If the writer were to go and live in the 'Free' State, he could apply for and obtain letters of exemption from the ordinary pass laws; but if his wife, who has had a better schooling and enjoyed an older civilisation than he, were to go and reside in the 'Free' State with her daughters, all of them would be forced to carry passes on their persons, and be called upon to ransack their skirt pockets at anytime in the public streets at the behest of male policemen in quest of their passes.

3. By **Philip Ochieng'** in the *Sunday Nation* of 10 August 2003.

It stands to commonsense, Aids is basically a health matter. The National Aids Control Council (NACC) should thus report to the Ministry of Health. Yet, consider the counter-argument, NACC's concerns go far beyond health issues.

Therefore, it is better handled by an office which cuts across all ministries. And the President's Office (OP) takes the case. B-right-o! But let us broaden the issue a little; is there any governance task which lies beyond the *nation's health*? Not that I know of. The nation cannot survive on aspirins, syringes and condoms alone.

No hospital can cure a plethora of other viruses that afflict us. When Simeon Nyachae declares that our economy is in the intensive care unit, is it an empty metaphor? When our economy is dead – as it already is for millions – of what use will Charity Ngilu's antibiotics be?

Our cities are decomposed, our dwellings dilapidated, our roads impassable, our agriculture sterile, our industry laughable, our schools rundown, our teachers ignorant, our politicians decayed, our homes broken, our children delinquent, our priests very like the Pharisees who took to Jesus a woman caught in the act.

Thus, the economic abyss is vitally linked to our mental illness. Because we pursue purely individual vegetable desires, we completely ignore "the common good". So we kill one another, rob one another, starve one another, rape one another, malign one another, are rude to one another.

Only depravity can allow a person to live on Olympus – his conscience at peace with all below – when his siblings die in excruciating hunger. Only mental degradation will allow one to gorge oneself like shoats when millions of one's compatriots are as emaciated as Pharaoh's kine.

From malaria to incivility, from corruption to Aids, this is the social ill health by which the Government justifies its existence. Every ministry purports to be delivering us from the stench of its putrescence.

Every ministry, then – if it were genuine – would consider itself a health ministry and discharging its particular mandate only in relation to the mandates of the ministries, with the OP as the queen health ministry. Only thus networked can they give a holistic solution to our national malaise.

If Mrs. Ngilu thinks she can cure us with pills alone – if the ministry does not predicate medication on food, water, roads, electricity, industry, trade, employment, teachers and the environment – it is a waste of time and money.

4. *Of Studies* from the *Essays* of Francis Bacon 1597 (spelling modernised)

Studies serve for delight, for ornament, and for ability. Their chief use for delight is in privateness and retiring; for ornament, is in discourse; and for ability, is in the judgement and disposition of business. For expert men can execute, and perhaps judge of particulars, one by one; but the general counsels, and the plots, and marshalling of affairs, come best from those that are learned. To spend too much time in studies, is sloth; to use them too much for ornament, is affectation; to make judgement wholly by their rules is the humour of a scholar. They perfect nature, and are perfected by experience: for natural abilities are like natural plants, that need pruning by study: and studies themselves do give forth directions too much at large, except they be bounded in by experience. Crafty men condemn studies; simple men admire them; and wise men use them; for they teach not their own use; but that is wisdom without them, and above them, taught by observation. Read not to contradict, and confute; nor to believe and take for granted; nor to find talk and discourse; but to weigh and consider. Some books are to be tasted, others to be swallowed, and some few to be chewed and digested...

Reading maketh a full man: conference a ready man; and writing an exact man.

The Analysis

The passage from *Bacon's essays* is typical of his witty and balanced style. The original is full of capital letters. The punctuation is very far from the modern logical style: this is in itself an interesting aspect of the historical study of written English.

Bacon, who claimed to "take all knowledge for his province", was a well-known philosopher and scholar but could not resist the lure of politics, and got involved in many controversies. These contradictions are reflected in the attitude of the passage, which nevertheless has some useful points to make.

The *Philip Ochieng' piece* is elegant in the classic way. The points are rammed home with impeccable logic. The choice of words and grammatical forms is exact. The local situation is placed firmly in a world-wide thought context – the Greek gods high on Mount Olympus, Pharaoh's dream of the fat and lean cattle, described in the words of the authorised version of the Bible, and the woman taken in adultery. Ochieng' respects his readers enough to assume they will pick up the references. Even the B of *B*-right-o.

The marvellously crafted piece by *Daniachew Worku* is more ambitious, though it depends on the sustained interplay of landscape, attitude and ritual in the novel about the pilgrimage taken to seek healing for the narrator's father according to Ethiopian Christian custom. I have not been able to find any other work in English by this fine writer. Notice that he often disregards formal sentence structure, building up the picture by additional phrases within full stops, in apposition to the main statement, that is, in such close association with it that the reader can fill in for himself the repeated grammatical forms. "There a saddle cloth flapping in the wind" and so on. These are adverbial phrases which could be attached by a comma to the sentence ending with the word mule, if they were not so many of them. The writer does not waste time simplifying: we have all seen pictures of horses and mules in harness, if not the real thing, and if we badly want to know which is the crupper and which the girth, a dictionary will tell us.

The apparently casual reference to protecting the mule from the evil eye links this descriptive passage to the main thrust of the story. The priests' song is linked with a cry of dread. The chief's overshirt of rich embroidered fabric is worn with a hat of straw and grass. Irony and paradox underlie every simple statement.

The passage from *Sol Plaatje* shows how an accomplished journalist can adopt the idiom of the time in whatever language he is writing: he was said to have command of three Europeans and six African languages. His fluency and echo of idioms and jokes in the English vein – for instance, the poem about roasting coffee – suggest how different things might have been in South Africa without the Act of Union. However, he is aware too of protesters amongst the Afrikaner farmers and can also (in other passages) imitate their conversational style. He seems unembarrassed by the word "native" as bringing together African and coloured citizens of many different communities: he is quick to point out that his wife was from an area with an older tradition of Western education than the Tswana, and he seems more concerned with social status than with "homelands."

Exercises

1. Translate the Chinua Achebe sentence quoted in Chapter one into Swahili or your mother-tongue. If you are working in a group, compare the versions, especially noting how many clauses they contain.

2. Write a chapter of the novel proposed in Chapter 4. If you are in a group, choose different segments of the story and note what adaptations you need to make to carry forward the characterisation each of you has proposed through all the episodes. You may end up with a version for each of the methods outlined in the text.

3. Select

   • a reflective essay from a recent newspaper
   • a textbook account of a historical event
   • a short episode from Ngugi's *Petals of Blood*
   • an episode from a novel of Dickens, for example Pip's first meeting with the convict in *Great Expectations*.

   Compare and contrast these in terms of:

   o style
   o address to the reader
   o independence or dependence in terms of outside information
   o emotional impact or satisfaction.

4. "It is November 1904, in Ohio. You are a passenger on the Dayton-Spring-Field-Urbana branch line. As your steam train passes a substantial area of scrubland known as the Huffman Prairie, you are aware of a loud clattering mechanical noise, rather like reaper. Looking out of the window, you see something wholly extraordinary.

    "Climbing slowly into the air is a huge flying machine with two wings, two propellers, a tail and an elevator at the front. There is a man lying astride the lower wing... the machine banks and turns with absolute stability."

    Describe your reaction in a newspaper report. Localise it to Kenya if you wish.

    (This was the plane used by the brothers Orville and Wilbur Wright operating less than a year after their first flight of 120 feet. The description is by William Boyd in the *Times Literary Supplement* of 30 May, 2003).

References

Achebe, Chinua. *Anthills of the Savanna.* London: Heinemann, 1987.

Akare, T. *The Slums.* Nairobi: Heinemann-AWS, 1981.

Amadi, E. *The Concubine.* London: Heinemann-AWS, 1966.

Armah, A.K. *Two Thousand Seasons.* Nairobi: EA Publishing House, 1973.

Austen, Jane. *Pride and Prejudice.* 1813. Harmondsworth: Penguin, 1994.

_____. *Sense and Sensibility.* 1811. Harmondsworth: Penguin, 1994.

_____. *Mansfield Park.* 1814. Harmondsworth: Penguin, 1994.

_____. *Emma.* 1816. Harmondsworth: Penguin, 1994.

_____. *Persuasion.*1818. Harmondsworth: Penguin, 1994.

_____. *Northanger Abbey.* 1818. Harmondsworth: Penguin, 1994.

Authors and Printers Dictionary ed. Collins. London: Oxford U. P., 1978.

Banville, J. *The Untouchable.* New York: Knopf, 1997.

Bronte, Emily. *Wuthering Heights.* 1847. Harmondsworth: Penguin, 1946.

Broomfield, G.W. *Hekaya za Abunuwasi na Hadithi Nyingine.* Macmillan, 1996 edition.

Bunyan, John. *Pilgrim's Progress.* Many editions.

Burgess, A. *The Novel Now.* London: Faber, 1967.

Burton, R. *The Anatomy of Melancholy.* 1621, Many editions.

Byatt, A.S. *Possession.* New York: Vintage, 1990.

Camus, A. *The Myth of Sisyphus.* (English) London: H. Hamilton, 1955.

Carey, P. *Oscar and Lucinda.* London: Faber, 1988.

Carnegie, Dale. *How to Make Friends and Influence People.* London: World's Work, 1938.

Cheney-Coker, S. *The Last Harmattan of Alisoune Dunbar.* London: Heinemann-AWS, 1990.

Coetzee, J.M. *Life and Times of Michael K.* London: Secker, 1983, Penguin, 1985.

Collins, Wilkie. *The Woman in White,* 1860, Harmondsworth: Penguin, 1994.

Dickens, Charles. *Bleak House.* 1853, Harmondsworth: Penguin, 1971 and many other editions.

_____. *A Tale of Two Cities.* 1850. Harmondsworth: Penguin, 1994.

_____. *Great Expectations.* 1851. Harmondsworth: Penguin, 1971.

_____. *Our Mutual Friend.* 1864. Harmondsworth: Penguin, 1971.

Donne, John. *Poems.* London: Dent-Everyman, 1931.

Dostoevsky, F. *Crime and Punishment,* 1866. Translated with an introduction by David Magarshack. Harmondsworth: Penguin, 1990.

_____. *The Idiot.* 1868. Harmondsworth: Penguin, 1955.

Dumas, A. *The Count of Monte Cristo.* 1845. Many editions.

Ellison, R. *The Invisible Man.* New York: Random House, 1952.

Farah, N. *From a Crooked Rib.* London: Heinemann-AWS, 1979, Harmondsworth: Penguin, 1990.

Faulkner, W. *The Sound and the Fury.* 1929. Harmondsworth: Penguin, 2005.

Ford, F. Madox *The Fifth Queen,* London: Bodley Head, 1906/8. Everyman-plc, 1991.

_____. *The Good Soldier.* London: Bodley Head, 1915, London Everyman-D. Campbell, 1991.

Geteria, Wamugunda. *Black Gold of Chepkube*. E.A.E.P Nairobi: 1985.

Gibbon, E. The Decline and Fall of the Roman Empire. 1776-1788. Many editions.

Golding, W. *The Lord of the Flies*. London: Faber, 1954.

_____. *The Spire*. London: Faber, 1964.

Gosse, E. *Father and Son*. 1907. Harmondsworth: Penguin.

Green, Henry. *Living (1929), Loving (1945), Party-Going (1939)*. Combined edition, London: Picador, 1978.

Greene, Graham. *Brighton Rock*. 1938. Everyman-D. Campbell, 1995.

_____. *The Power and the Glory*. London: Bodley Head, 1940.

Hawthorne, N. *The Scarlet Letter*. 1850 London: Oxford U.P. – America Classics, 1965.

Heller, J. *Catch 22*. 1961 London: Everyman-D. Campbell, 1995.

Hobbes, T. *Leviathan*. 1651. Harmondsworth: Penguin.

Hughes, R. *A High Wind in Jamaica*. Harmondsworth: Penguin, (1929); c. 1938.

Hutchinson, R. C. *Recollection of a Journey*. London: Cassell-Zenith, 1952.

Imbuga, F. *Shrine of Tears*. Nairobi: Longman, 1993.

Ishiguro, K. *When we Were Orphans*. London: Faber, 2000.

Joyce, J. *Ulysses*. 1922. Paris: Shakespeare Press. London: Bodley Head, 1936.

Kahiga, S. *Dedan Kimathi, The Real Story*. Nairobi: Longman, 1990.

_____. *Paradise Farm*. Nairobi: Longman, 1993.

Kipling, R. *Kim*. London: Macmillan, 1901.

Kurtz, J.R. *Urban Obsessions, Urban Fears: The Post-Colonial Kenyan Novel*. Trenton N.J. AWP: and Oxford: James Currey, 1998.

Lamming, C. *In the Castle of my Skin*. London: M. Joseph, 1953.

Lawrence, D.H. *Women in Love*. London: Heinemann, 1921.

_____. *Lady Chatterley's Lover*. London: Heinemann, 1928.

_____. *Sons and Lovers*. London: Heinemann, 1913.

Laye, C. *The African (Dark) Child*. Fr. 1953, Eng. Tr. J. Kirkup, London: Collins, 1955.

Le Carre, John. *The Constant Gardener*. London: Hutchinson, 2001.

Lefanu, S. & Hayward, S. *Colours of a New Day*. Johannesburg: Raven Press, 1990.

McCarthy, C. *The Orchard Keeper*. 1965. London: Picador, 1994.

Malamud, B. *The Fixer*. New York: Farrar Strauss, 1966.

Malthus, T. *An Essay on Population*. 1798, Many editions.

Maran, R. *Bataoula*. 1921. Eng. Tr. London: Heinemann-AWS, 1973.

Marquez, G.G. *One Hundred Years of Solitude*. 1967 Eng. New York: Harper Row, 1970.

Melville, H. *Moby Dick*. 1851. Many editions.

Mendelsohn, D. in *New York Review of Books*, 13 May, 2004.

Mitchell, M. *Gone with the Wind*. New York: 1936.

Moliere. *Le Bourgeois Gentilhomme*. 1670 Many editions.

Moore, G. *Esther Waters*. 1894. Many editions.

Morrison, Toni. *Beloved*. London: Chatto and Windus, 1987.

Mungoshi, C. *Waiting for the Rain*. London: Heinemann-AWS, 1975.

Mutahi, Wahome. *Three Days on the Cross-*. Nairobi: E.A.E.P, 1991.

_____*The Jail Bugs*. Nairobi: Longhorn, 1992.

Mwangi, Meja. *The Last Plague*. Nairobi: E.A.E.P, 2000.

_____*The Return of Shaka*. Nairobi: Longhorn, 1989.

_____*Carcase for Hounds*. Nairobi: E.A.P.H, 1974, reprinted E.A.E.P.

Naipaul, V.S. *A House for Mr. Biswas*. London: A. Deutsch, 1961.

Napoleon's Book of Fate. London: Foulsham, no date.

Ngugi wa Thiong'o. *The River Between*. London: Heinemann-AWS, 1963.

_____. *Petals of Blood*. London: Heinemann-AWS, 1972.

_____. *A Grain of Wheat*. London: Heinemann-AWS, 1968.

Njau, Rebeka. *The Sacred Seed*. Nairobi: Books Horizon, 2003.

Nkrumah, Kwame. *Black Star*. London: Nelson, 1957.

Ogola, M. *The River and the Source*. Nairobi: Focus Books, 1993.

Ogot, Grace A. *Land Without Thunder*. Nairobi: E.A.P.H., 1968, reprinted E.A.E.P.

_____. *The Strange Bride*. Nairobi: Heinemann, 1989.

Oludhe-Macgoye, M. *Coming to Birth*. London: W. Heinemann and Nairobi: E.A.E.P., 1986.

_____. *The Present Moment*. London: W. Heinemann and Nairobi: E.A.E.P., 1987.

_____. *Homing In*. Nairobi: E.A.E.P., 1993.

_____. *Chira*. Nairobi: E.A.E.P., 1997.

_____. *Street Life*. Nairobi: E.A.E.P., 1988.

_____. *The Black Hand Gang*. Nairobi: E.A.E.P., 1997.

_____. *Victoria & Murder in Majengo*. Basingstoke: Macmillan, 1993.

Ondaatje, M. *The English Patient*. London: Bloomsbury, 1992.

Orwell, G. *Animal Farm*. 1945, Harmondsworth: Penguin and other editions.

_____. *1984*. 1949, Harmondsworth: Penguin and other editions.

Parks, T. in *New York Review of Books*, 25 September 2003.

Pasternak, B. *Dr. Zhivago*. (Eng.), London: Collins and Harvill, 1957.

Plaatje, Sol. *Mhudi*. London: Heinemann-AWS, 1978.

_____. *Native Life in South Africa*. 1916, London: Longman 1987.

Priestley, J.B. *The Good Companions*. London: Heinemann, 1929.

Pynchon, T. *Gravity's Rainbow*. New York: Viking, 1973.

Rao, Raja. *Kathnapoori*. Delhi: Orient Paperbacks.

Rhys, J. *The Wide Sargasso Sea*, 2ND ed. London: Hodder and Stoughton, 1989.

Rushdie, S. *Midnight's Children*, New York: Knopf, 1980.

Sayers, Dorothy. *The Nine Tailors*. London: Gollancz, 1934.

Scott, Paul. *The Birds of Paradise*. London: Heinemann, 1962.

_____. *The Jewel in the Crown*. London: Heinemann, 1966.

_____. ed. S.C Reece. *My Appointment with the Muse*, London: Heinemann, 1986.

Shenk, D. *Justice, Reconciliation and Peace in Africa*. Nairobi: Uzima Press.

Shorter Cambridge History of English Literature. Cambridge: Cambridge University Press, 1940.

Smith, Adam. *The Wealth of Nations*. 1776, Harmondsworth Penguin.

Steinbeck, J. *The Grapes of Wrath*. 1939.

Sterne, L. *Tristram Shandy*. 1767, London: Everyman, 1991.

Stevenson, R.L. *Treasure Island*. 1883. Harmondsworth: Penguin, 1994.

_____. *Dr. Jekyll and Mr. Hyde*. 1886. Harmondsworth: Penguin, 1994.

Stowe, H.B. *Uncle Tom's Cabin*. 1852. Many editions.

Styron, W. *The Confessions of Nat Turner*. New York: Random House, 1966.

Thackeray, W.M. *Vanity Fair*, 1847, Harmondsworth: Penguin, 1994.

Tolkien, J.R. *Lord of the Rings*, combined edition, London: Allen and Unwin, 1969.

Traherne, T. *Centuries of Meditations*. London: Dobson, 1908.

Wain, John. in *Word in the Desert, Critical Quarterly 10th Anniversary Issue*. London: Oxford UP, 1969.

West, R. *The Fountain Overflows*. London: Macmillan, 1937.

White, P. *Voss*. London: Eyre & Spottiswoode, 1957, Harmondsworth: Penguin, 1960.

____. *Flaws in the Glass: a Self-portrait*. London: Cape, 1981.
Harmondsworth: Penguin, 1983.

____. *The Tree of Man*. London: Eyre and Spottiswoode, 1956.

Wicomb, Z. in Lefanu, S. & S. Hayward. *Colours of a New Day*.
Johannesburg: Raven Press, 1990.

Index